PEARSON LONGMAN

CORNERSTONE

2

PEARSON English Learning System

Anna Uhl Chamot

Jim Cummins

Sharroky Hollie

PEARSON

Upper Saddle River, New Jersey • Boston, Massachusetts • Chandler, Arizona • Glenview, Illinois

Pearson Longman Cornerstone 2

PEARSON English Learning System

Staff credits: The people who made up the Longman Cornerstone team, representing editorial, production, design, manufacturing, and marketing, are John Ade, Rhea Banker, Virginia Bernard, Daniel Comstock, David Dickey, Gina DiLlillo, Johnnie Farmer, Nancy Flaggman, Charles Green, Karen Kawaguchi, Ed Lamprich, Niki Lee, Jaime Leiber, Chris Leonowicz, Tara Maceyak, Linda Moser, Laurie Neaman, Leslie Patterson, Sherri Pemberton, Diane Pinkley, Liza Pleva, Susan Saslow, Chris Siley, Loretta Steeves, Kim Steiner, and Lauren Weidenman.

Text design and composition: The Quarasan Group, Inc.
Illustration and photo credits appear on page 365, which constitute an extension of this copyright page.

Library of Congress Cataloging-in-Publication Data
Chamot, Anna Uhl.
    Longman Cornerstone / Anna Uhl Chamot, Jim Cummins, Sharroky Hollie.
    p. cm. — (Longman Cornerstone)
    Includes index.
    1. Language arts (Elementary school)—United States. 2. Language arts
(Elementary school)—Activity programs 3. English language—Study and teaching.
    I. Cummins, Jim II. Hollie, Sharroky III. Title.

ISBN-13: 978-1-4284-3473-8
ISBN-10: 1-4284-3473-9

Printed in the United States of America
4 5 6 7 8 9 10 V057 16 15 14

Anna Uhl Chamot is a professor of secondary education and a faculty advisor for ESL in George Washington University's Department of Teacher Preparation. She has been a researcher and teacher trainer in content-based second-language learning and language-learning strategies. She co-designed and has written extensively about the Cognitive Academic Language Learning Approach (CALLA) and spent seven years implementing the CALLA model in the Arlington Public Schools in Virginia.

Jim Cummins is the Canada Research Chair in the Department of Curriculum, Teaching, and Learning of the Ontario Institute for Studies in Education at the University of Toronto. His research focuses on literacy development in multilingual school contexts, as well as on the potential roles of technology in promoting language and literacy development. His recent publications include: *The International Handbook of English Language Teaching* (co-edited with Chris Davison) and *Literacy, Technology, and Diversity: Teaching for Success in Changing Times* (with Kristin Brown and Dennis Sayers).

Sharroky Hollie is an assistant professor in teacher education at California State University, Dominguez Hills. His expertise is in the field of professional development, African-American education, and second-language methodology. He is an urban literacy visiting professor at Webster University, St. Louis. Sharroky is the Executive Director of the Center for Culturally Responsive Teaching and Learning (CCRTL) and the co-founding director of the nationally-acclaimed Culture and Language Academy of Success (CLAS).

Consultants and Reviewers

Rebecca Anselmo
Sunrise Acres Elementary School
Las Vegas, NV

Ana Applegate
Redlands School District
Redlands, CA

Terri Armstrong
Houston ISD
Houston, TX

Jacqueline Avritt
Riverside County Office of Ed.
Hemet, CA

Mitchell Bobrick
Palm Beach County School
West Palm Beach, FL

Victoria Brioso-Saldala
Broward County Schools
Fort Lauderdale, FL

Brenda Cabarga Schubert
Creekside Elementary School
Salinas, CA

Joshua Ezekiel
Bardin Elementary School
Salinas, CA

Veneshia Gonzalez
Seminole Elementary School
Okeechobee, FL

Carolyn Grigsby
San Francisco Unified School District
San Francisco, CA

Julie Grubbe
Plainfield Consolidated Schools
Chicago, IL

Yasmin Hernandez-Manno
Newark Public Schools
Newark, NJ

Janina Kusielewicz
Clifton Public Schools/Bilingual Ed.
& Basic Skills Instruction Dept.
Clifton, NJ

Mary Helen Lechuga
El Paso ISD
El Paso, TX

Gayle P. Malloy
Randolph School District
Randolph, MA

Randy Payne
Patterson/Taft Elementaries
Mesa, AZ

Marcie L. Schnegelberger
Alisal Union SD
Salinas, CA

Lorraine Smith
Collier County Schools
Naples, FL

Shawna Stoltenborg
Glendale Elementary School
Glen Burnie, MD

Denise Tiffany
West High School
Iowa City, IO

Dear Student,

Welcome to *Longman Cornerstone*!

We wrote *Longman Cornerstone* to help you learn to read, write, and speak English. We wrote a book that will make learning English and learning to read a lot of fun.

Cornerstone includes a mix of all subjects. We have written some make-believe stories and some true stories.

As you use this program, you will build on what you already know, learn new words and new information, and take part in projects. The projects will help you improve your English skills.

Learning a language takes time, but just like learning to swim or ride a two-wheeler, it is fun!

We hope you enjoy *Longman Cornerstone* as much as we enjoyed writing it for you!

Good luck!

Anna Uhl Chamot
Jim Cummins
Sharroky Hollie

Contents

Families

Reading 3

Put It All Together

Growing Up

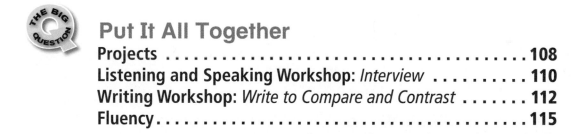

What We Like

Reading 1

Reading 2

Then and Now

Plants and Animals

Reading 3

Put It All Together

Different Places

Unit 1

Families

People in families live together and help one another. How do the people in your family help one another? Tell the class.

THE BIG Q QUESTION

What do families do together on special days?

VIEW AND RESPOND

DVD *Watch the video. What is it about?*

Talk about the poster. What does it show?

Visit LongmanCornerstone.com.

What Do You Know about Families?

Use what you know to help you understand.

Parents teach their children.

Everyone helps.

4

Families live
in homes.

Children learn new things.

Your Turn

How do you
help at home?
Tell the class
about it.

Sing about Families

Family Fun

There are mothers and dads. It's true!

There are sisters and brothers, too.

Aunts and uncles and cousins care.

Grandmas and grandpas are everywhere.

So it's a grand time to celebrate.

It's a grand time to play.

So sing, eat, chat and have fun
with your family today.

Reading Tip

We read English
from left to right
and from top to
bottom.

7

Two Syllable Words

The word *children* is a **two syllable** word.

chil – dren

Say the word.

Say the two syllables. Point to each syllable as you say it.

Rule

Each syllable has one vowel sound. Some vowel sounds are spelled with more than one letter.

yel - low   trail - er

Your Turn

**Work with a partner.
Take turns.**

Read the passage aloud:

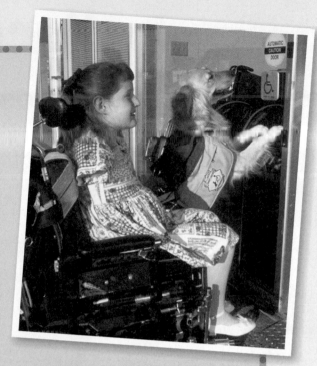

I took my puppy for
a walk to town. We
saw lots of shops.
I wanted to buy a pencil for me and
some ribbon for my mom. I saw
a yellow candle that was very pretty.
I bought the candle. I will get the
pencil and the ribbon the next time
I go to the store.

- Which words have two syllables?

- How do you know?

- List the words in your notebook.

Vocabulary

Words to Know

1. I like to sing.

These words
will help you
understand the
reading.

2. There are a lot
   of choices. What
   will Matt buy
   to eat?

Sight Words

sing

are

buy

eat

3. I wash the dog.
   I clean him up.
   It is my chore.

Story Words

wash

clean

chore

Your Turn

Pick one word from either box.

Use the word in a sentence.

Ask your teacher if you need help.

3

10

Phonics

Phonics

a

Short a; Consonants

Read the words aloud. Listen for the letter sounds.

map

ax

ant

bag

Your Turn

Which letter stands for the sound at the beginning of the word?

t c d   a p l   n f h   h t a

Story Preview

Who is in the story?

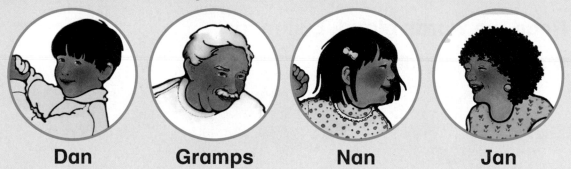

Dan   **Gramps**   **Nan**   **Jan**

What is the story about?

Dan and Gramps have chores to do.

Reading Strategy

Find the Main Idea

The main idea is the most important idea in the story.
Look for the main idea as you read.

Dan and Gramps

by Pam Walker

illustrated by N. Jo Tufts

Dan has a chore. Gramps has
a chore. Dan and Gramps can fold
the wash.

Dan and Gramps can sing .
Dan and Gramps can clean . Dan
and Gramps can sing and clean.

Gramps has a bag of soap. Dan
can wash a sock. Dan and Gramps
can wash and clean.

Gramps can buy a ham. Gramps
can buy yams.

Dan can grab a bag. The bag has
cans and jam. Dan's bag is full.

Gramps and Jan and Sam
can eat. Dan has a pal, Nan. Gramps
and Dan are glad.

Think It Over

Audio **Listen to the questions and say the answers. Use Sight Words and Story Words.**

1. Who has a chore?

2. What day is it? How do you know?

3. What can Dan and Gramps do?

4. What do you do on Saturdays?

Speaking Tip

Look at the pictures from the story again. Retell the story.

Reading Strategy

Find the Main Idea

What is the main idea of the story?

5–6

A Closer Look at... Grocery Stores

Audio

◀ Samples

This boy samples food in a grocery store.

Vegetables ▶

This family buys fresh vegetables.

Grocery Cart ▶
This family
puts things in
a grocery cart.

▲ **Labels**
This family reads
food labels.

Activity to Do

These two pages use pictures and
words to tell about grocery stores.

- Think of another kind of store.
- Find pictures to show that store.
- Talk about your pictures with
  the class.

21

Grammar and Writing

Can + Verb

Use *can* + **verb** to talk about things someone is able to do.

Use *cannot* or *can't* + **verb** for things someone is not able to do.

I **can play** basketball.

I **cannot swim**.

To ask a question, use *can* + subject + **verb**.

Can he **ride** a bike?

No, he **cannot ride** a bike well.

Add _can_ or _can't_. Write the sentences.

Example: <u>Can</u> you sing? No, <u>I can't</u>.

1. ___ your brother ride a bike? No, he ___.

2. ___ Louisa do her chores? Yes, she ___.

3. ___ cats play basketball? No, they ___.

4. ___ the baby clean his room? No, he ___.

Ask and answer questions. Use words in the box.

Example: A: Can you dance well?

         B: Yes, I can.

> play basketball
> ride a bike
> swim

Write about what you _can_ and _can't_ do.

>   I can sing and ride a bike.
> I can read well. I can swim well.
> I can't dance.

WB

7–8

23

Vocabulary

Words to Know

1. I will give the big box to Dad. It feels too heavy. I do not want to get hurt.

These words will help you understand the reading.

Sight Words

give

big

feels

hurt

Story Words

learn

parents

children

2. We learn from Mom.

3. Parents teach their children.

Your Turn

Pick one word from either box.

Use the word in a sentence.

9

24

Phonics

Short e; th

Read the words aloud. Listen for the letter sounds.

bed

egg

bath

pen

WB PH

10

Your Turn

Write the missing letter or letters.

j ___ t

b ___ ll

$\begin{array}{r} 2 \\ +3 \\ \hline 5 \end{array}$

ma ___

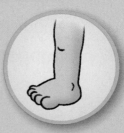

l ___ g

25

Story Preview

What is the story about?

Parents and others help children learn.

Reading Strategy

Cause and Effect

A cause is why something happens. An effect is what happens as a result of a cause. Look for causes and effects as you read.

Shared Reading Your teacher will show you how to use the strategy. Listen, watch, and practice.

Children Can Learn

by Dan White

Glen is a small baby. Mom and Dad help Glen. Dad can give Glen a bottle. Glen can be fed. Then Glen can get a nap.

Nell is not big yet. Nell is small. Nell gets help. Mom can help Nell. She can give Nell a snack.

Can Bess get milk? Yes, but Bess makes a mess. Bess feels bad. Bess can ask Dad to help.

Dad can help Bess. Dad is glad
to help Bess. Bess can get milk. Bess
feels good. Bess and Dad are glad.
Bess tells Dad, "Thanks!"

Dan can learn math. Dan has a math test. Dan gets help to pass the math test.

Dad can help Jan spell hen, pen, den, bell, and well. Dad helps Jan spell and pass a test.

Parents help children. Matt can get hurt. Mom helps Matt.

Matt is safe. Matt will not get hurt.

Fred has a red bat. Dad can help Fred hit a ball. Fred can run fast.

Fred tells Dad, "Thanks." Fred is glad Dad can help.

Think It Over

Listen to the questions and say the answers. Use Sight Words and Story Words.

1. How do Mom and Dad help Glen?

2. How does Mom help Matt?

3. Why is Fred glad Dad can help?

4. What do you learn from your mom and dad?

Speaking Tip

If you don't understand, ask a partner a question about the story.

11–12

Reading Strategy

Cause and Effect

What causes and effects did you find in the story?

Grammar and Writing

Simple Present

Use the simple present to talk about things that happen all the time. For **he**, **she**, and **it**, add **-s** after the verb. To make a negative sentence, use **do not** or **does not** before the verb.

> I **play** in the park on Sundays.
> My sister **rides** her bike.
> She **does not play** in the park.

To ask a question, use **do** or **does** + subject + **verb**.

> **Do** I **play** in the park?
> Yes, I **do**.

> **Does** my sister **play** with me?
> No, she **doesn't**.

> do not = **don't**
> does not = **doesn't**

36

Add *do*, *don't*, *does*, or *doesn't*. Write the sentences.

Example: Do you swim at the gym? No, I don't.

1. ___ your father watch TV? Yes, he ___.

2. ___ your parents listen to music? No, they ___.

3. ___ you eat a big dinner on Sundays? Yes, we ___.

4. ___ your sister give the dog a bath? Yes, she ___.

5. ___ your brother like pizza? No, he ___.

Get in a group. Talk about your family and friends.

Example: A: Does your brother play soccer?

          B: No, he doesn't. He plays basketball.

Write about a friend or a family member.

My sister takes dance lessons on Saturdays. Sometimes she plays cards with my brother. She also uses the computer.

Vocabulary

Words to Know

These words will help you understand the reading.

1. Mel's house is yellow. It has five rooms. Mel does not have his own room.

2. Jed does not live in a house. He lives in a big apartment.

3. We live in a long trailer.

Sight Words

yellow

five

does

own

Story Words

house

apartment

trailer

15

38

Your Turn

Pick one word from either box.

Use the word in a sentence.

Phonics

Short i; sh

Read the words aloud. Listen for the letter sounds.

dig

ship

ill

ink

WB | PH

16

Your Turn

Write the missing letter or letters.

l ___ ps

sw ___ m

fi ___

p ___ g

39

Story Preview

Who are some people in the story?

Ned and Dad

Jen, Jim, and Mom

What is the story about?

People live in different kinds of homes.

Reading Strategy

Predict

When you predict, you guess what is going to happen in a story. Use the drawings, the title, and other clues to help you predict.

40

We Live in a Home

by Anya Hansen

illustrated by Elliot Kreloff

Get up! Get out of bed! Tell us where
you live. Let us see!

Jen and Jim live in an apartment in town. It has steps.

Jen wants a big pet, but the pet will not fit. Jim wants a fish. The fish is little. Mom does not want a pet.

Ted and Pam live in a yellow trailer. Ted and Pam have a pet. The pet is a black cat named Tisha. Ted and Pam tell Tisha to be good when they leave. Tisha likes to play with a ball of yarn. Do you think Tisha will be good?

Ned and Dad have their own houseboat.
It has a deck where they can sit in the sun. A
houseboat is a boat and a place to live. Today the
weather will be hot. Do you think Ned and Dad
will swim?

Mom and Dad live in a house. Five people can fit in the house. It has a den and a desk. The house is red and yellow.

Get in bed, Jen and Jim. Get in bed, Ted and Pam. Go to sleep, Tisha.

Get in bed, Ned and Dad. Get in bed, Mom and Dad. Get in bed and go to sleep.

Think It Over

Listen to the questions and say the answers. Use Sight Words and Story Words.

1. Where do Jen and Jim live?

2. What is Ted and Pam's home like?

3. Where do Ned and Dad live?

4. Which home in the story is most like your home?

WB

17–18

Reading Strategy

Predict

How did predicting help you understand what you read?

49

Grammar and Writing

Be Verbs

The *be* verbs are *am, is,* and *are*. *Be* verbs need to agree with the person, place, or thing you are talking about.

> I **am** a teacher.
> It **is** Friday.
> He **is** Tom.
> She **is** Maria.
> They **are** my students.
> We **are** in class.
> You **are** in class, too.

To say something is not true, put *not* after *am, is,* or *are.* You can use the contractions of *is not* and *are not.*

> Maria **is not** a teacher.
> Maria and Tom **are not** teachers.

> is not = **isn't**
> are not = **aren't**

To make a question, put *am, is*, or *are* before the name for the person, place, or thing.

> Where **am** I?   What **are** they?   When **is** it?

Add *am*, *is*, or *are*. Write the sentences.

Example: I <u>am</u> glad.

1. They ___ my parents.

2. He ___ my big brother.

3. We ___ at home.

4. ___ they your books?

5. Who ___ I?

6. Our house ___ new.

Apply

Draw your family. Ask and answer questions about your pictures.

Example: A: Who is she?

                B: She's my mother.

Write

Write about the picture of your family.

> This is my family. They are my parents. He is my little brother. His name is Juan. He is five. He can read some words.

W B
19–20

What do families do together on special days? Talk about it.

Your teacher will help you choose one of these projects.

Written

Write about a special day.

Write a story to tell about a special day you had with your family.

Oral

Tell about a special day.

Share your special day with the class. Tell what you did with your family.

 ## Visual/Active

Draw your special day.

Draw pictures to show your special day with your family.

Story

Tell a story about something that happened to you.

① Prepare G.O. 109

Think about an event. What happened? What made the event interesting? Write the details in a chart like this:

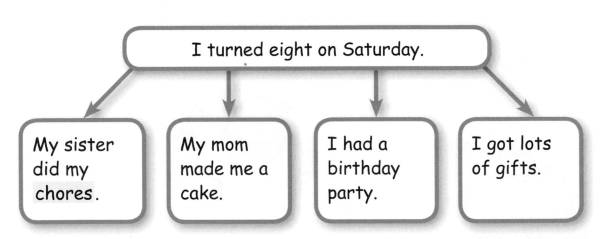

I turned eight on Saturday.

| My sister did my chores. | My mom made me a cake. | I had a birthday party. | I got lots of gifts. |

② Practice and Present

Use the chart to tell your story to a partner. Practice until you can tell the story without help. Then tell your story to the class. Your classmates can give it a title.

As you speak, do this:

- Use both short and long sentences.
- Join short sentences using *and* or *but*.

As you listen, do this:

- Listen for words you know. This will help you understand the speaker.
- Watch the speaker's face and hands. They can tell you about hidden ideas.

③ Evaluate

Ask yourself these questions:

- Was my story interesting?
- Can I retell one of the stories I heard? What words would I use?

More Practice

Find a picture of an event that is new to you. Tell a partner the main points of the picture. Then tell some important details. Ask your partner to guess what the picture shows. Finally, show the picture to your partner. Have him or her name what it shows. Switch roles.

Write a Letter

Write a letter to a relative. Tell this person about something new that you can do.

1 **Prewrite** Choose a relative to write to. Think about what you would like to tell this person. Make a plan for your letter.

Marisol planned her letter like this:

> Date <u>May 12, 2011</u>
>
> Dear <u>Aunt Luisa</u>
>
> 1. <u>I can ride a bike</u>
>
> 2. <u>My bike is yellow</u>
>
> 3. <u>Milly rides with me</u>
>
> Love, <u>Marisol</u>

2 **Draft** Use your plan to help you write a first draft of your letter. Use new words from the unit.

3 **Revise** Read your draft. Use the Revising Checklist to correct errors. Then revise your draft.

Here is Marisol's letter.

May 12, 2011

Dear Aunt Luisa,

I can ride a bike! I have my own bike. It is big and yellow. I ride it on weekends and after scool. Milly rides with me. She watches me so I won't get hurt. Can you ride a bike?

Love, Marisol

57

4 **Edit** Trade papers with a partner to get feedback. Use the Editing Checklist.

5 **Publish** Make a clean copy of your final draft. Share it with the class.

Editing Checklist

✓ Negatives and contractions are used correctly.

✓ Each sentence begins with a capital letter.

✓ Each question ends with a question mark.

✓ All the details are related to the topic.

Spelling Tip

Follow this rule: After *Milly*, *ride* ends in -*s*: **Milly rides**. After *I*, *ride* does not end in -*s*: **I ride**.

For Each Reading...

1. Listen to the sentences.

2. Work in pairs. Take turns reading aloud for one minute. Count the number of words you read.

It is Saturday. Dan has a chore. Gramps has a	10
chore. They can fold the wash. Dan and Gramps	19
can clean and sing. They can wash and clean.	28
Dan and Gramps can buy a ham, yams, and jam.	38
They eat with Jan, Sam, and Nan. They are glad.	48

3. With your partner, find the words that slowed you down. Practice saying each word and then say the sentence each word is in. Take turns reading the text again. Count the number of words you read.

25–26

Growing Up

All living things change as they grow. Tell the class how you have changed since you were a baby.

THE BIG QUESTION

What do you want to be when you grow up?

VIEW AND RESPOND

Watch the video. What is it about?

Talk about the poster. What does it show?

Visit LongmanCornerstone.com.

What Do You Know about Growing Up? 🔊

Use what you know
to help you understand.

Living things grow up.

A bear cub grows up
to be a big bear.

A baby grows up
to be a teenager.

A seed grows
to be a flower.

Your Turn

Think of how you
will grow up. Tell
the class about it.

63

Sing about Growing Up

Growing Up

We all grow up, and we all change.

We grow to be boys and girls.

We learn new things as we grow

And help each other more.

Growing up is so much fun!

Growing up and learning.

Growing up is so much fun!

We want to grow and learn.

Reading Tip

We read English from left to right and from top to bottom.

Word Study

Compound Words

The word **campfire** is a **compound** word. It is made up of two smaller words, **camp** and **fire**.

cupcake	bedtime	sunrise
cup + cake	bed + time	sun + rise

Look for smaller words in larger words to help you say the larger words.

Rule

Look for the smaller words that make up compound words. This will help you find the meanings of the larger words.

$$back + pack = backpack$$

A **backpack** is a bag carried on your back.

Your Turn

Work with a partner. Take turns.

- Read each word below aloud.

- Look for the smaller words in each compound word to help you say the word.

- Tell what the word means.

    1. bookmark
    2. lunchroom
    3. rainbow
    4. sunflower
    5. homework
    6. jellyfish

Vocabulary

Words to Know

These words will help you understand the reading.

Sight Words

light

hold

him

funny

Story Words

year

puppy

grown-up

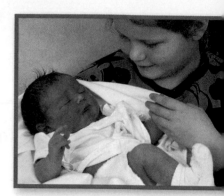

1. My new brother is light, so I can hold him. He makes funny faces.

2. In one year, this puppy will be a grown-up dog.

Your Turn

Pick one word from either box.

Use the word in a sentence.

Ask your teacher if you need help.

Phonics

Phonics

o

wh

Short o; wh

Read the words aloud. Listen for the letter sounds.

on

hop

whip

pot

WB PH

30

Your Turn

Which letter, or letters, stand for the sound at the beginning of the word?

o a r

ch r wh

b x o

wh l sh

69

Story Preview

Who is in the story?

Spot

boy

What is the story about?

The story is about a boy and his dog.

Reading Strategy

Identify Characters

Characters are the people or animals that the story is about. As you read the story, think about what happens to the characters.

Spot Is a Pal

by Tracey Baptiste

illustrated by Elizabeth Allen

This is me and Spot. I am five.
Spot is a puppy. Spot is light, and I
can hold him. Does my puppy eat
a lot? Yes, Spot does.

A year passes. Now Spot is not as small. Spot is big. Spot and I play a lot. We run and run and run. Spot and I have fun. Does Spot eat a lot? Yes, Spot does.

Spot and I are big, and I am six. I
have a cake and a hat. I have gifts from
Mom and Dad. Spot sits with me. Spot
is a funny pet.

Spot and I sit and grin. Now I cannot hold Spot. Spot is not as light. Spot and I play and learn tricks. Spot can do a lot of tricks. Spot can sit, stay, and beg.

Spot is a funny pet. I get a lick from Spot as a kiss. Spot is my best pal.

Another year passes. Spot is a
grown-up dog. I am not grown yet. I
am still a kid. I will be a big kid soon. I
can't wait to be a big kid. Spot will still
be my best pal.

Think It Over

Listen to the questions and say the answers. Use Sight Words and Story Words.

1. Who is Spot?

2. What do Spot and the boy do together?

3. How does Spot change by the end of the story?

4. How do puppies change as they grow?

WB
31–32

Reading Strategy

Identify Characters

How did identifying the characters help you understand the story?

Grammar and Writing

More Simple Present

Use the simple present to talk about things that happen all the time. For *he*, *she*, and *it*, add -*s* or -*es* after the verb. Add -*es* if the verb ends in *ch*, *sh*, *s*, *x*, or *z*.

We **watch** TV.
Ming **watches** movies.
I **watch** funny shows.
Dad **doesn't watch** TV.

watch ⟶ watch**es**
wash ⟶ wash**es**
pass ⟶ pass**es**

Use the words *what*, *when*, and *where* to ask questions. Use a question word + *do* or *does* + subject + verb.

What do you read?
When does he read?
Where do they read?

Practice

Add the verb. Write the sentences.

Example: Dad <u>washes</u> the car. (wash)

1. Dan ___ in an apartment. (live)

2. Miguel and Pablo ___ lunch together. (eat)

3. Pam ___ the news on TV. (watch)

4. We ___ dance lessons on Tuesdays. (take)

Apply

Interview a friend. Ask questions.

Example: What do you like ? (eat, play)

When do you eat ? (sleep, play)

Where do you eat ? (sleep, work)

Write

Tell about a friend.

Bao is seven years old. He likes baseball. He and I play in the park after school. Bao doesn't watch TV. He reads books about animals.

WB
33–34

Prepare to Read

Vocabulary

Audio

Words to Know

These words will help you understand the reading.

Sight Words

her

cry

left

away

Story Words

people

beautiful

swan

1. The mother bird feeds her babies. They cry when they want food.

2. There is one baby bird left. Soon it will fly away.

3. People like to watch this beautiful swan.

Your Turn

Pick two words from either box.

Point to pictures that show those words.

WB
35

Phonics

Short u; ch

Read the words aloud.
Listen for the letter sounds.

up

lunch

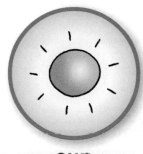

sun

hug

WB PH

36

Your Turn

Write the missing letter or letters.

b __ s

__ ick

t __ b

dr __ m

81

Story Preview

What is the story about?

This story is about a duckling that nobody likes.

Where does the story take place?

The story takes place at a duck's nest by the water.

Reading Strategy

Make Inferences

Sometimes a story does not tell you everything that happens. It gives you clues so that you can figure it out. As you read, look for clues in the story.

Shared Reading Your teacher will show you how to use the strategy. Listen, watch, and practice.

The Ugly Duckling

retold by Lauren Weidenman

illustrated by Helen Cann

Mama Duck sits on her nest, keeping
her eggs warm. At last, the eggs crack
open, and little ducklings come out.
"Peep, peep, peep!" they cry. "Are you all
out?" Mama Duck asks.

She checks her nest to find that there
is one egg left . It is big! Mama Duck sits
on her nest again, when suddenly, the
egg cracks. Out comes a BIG duckling.
"PEEP!" Mama Duck stares at him. He
does not look like the others.

Mama Duck takes her ducklings to the
farm. "What pretty little chicks!" cry
the geese. But they do not like the big
duckling. "He is ugly," they say; "we do
not want him here!"

The duckling is sad. Even his brothers
and sisters are not kind to him.
"Go away!" his sisters snap. "You are
ugly!" The poor duckling does not know
what to do. And so he runs away.

Fall comes and goes, and soon winter chills the air. The poor duckling shivers, cold and alone.

Spring brings the sun's warmth, turning the trees green. The duckling looks around and sees a swan. "How beautiful!" he cries. "I want to be like him." The duckling stretches his neck and bends his head down. "Oh! What is that in the water?"

He is not ugly. He is not a duckling. He is a swan! Other swans are his friends. People watch him swim, and children throw bread to him. He hears them say, "The new swan is the most beautiful of all." At last he belongs.

Think It Over

Audio

Listen to the questions and say the answers. Use Sight Words and Story Words.

1. Why is the duckling sad?

2. Why do the animals not like the duckling?

3. Why do the animals think the duckling is ugly?

4. What happens as animals and people grow up?

Speaking Tip

Look at the pictures from the story again. Retell the story.

37–38

Reading Strategy

Make Inferences

What does the duckling see in the water?

Fairy Tales

Wolf ▶

Little Red Riding Hood meets the wolf in her grandmother's house.

◀ **Tower**

Rapunzel lives in a tower and has long golden hair.

Stalk ▶

Jack gets beans that grow into a big stalk.

▲ **Mattress**

This princess can feel something as tiny as a pea under many mattresses.

Activity to Do

These pages use pictures and words to tell about fairy tales.

- Think of another fairy tale.
- Draw pictures to show what happens in that fairy tale.
- Talk about your pictures with the class.

Grammar and Writing

Subject and Object Pronouns

Sentences have subjects and verbs. The subject and verb always agree. Often sentences have an object after the verb.

subject	verb	object
People	like	ice cream.

A **pronoun** stands for a **noun**. Subject pronouns come before the verb.

subject

Oliva holds the baby boy.

She holds the baby boy.

Subject Pronouns

I, you, he, she, it, they, we

Object pronouns come after the verb.

object

Oliva holds **the baby boy.**

Oliva holds **him.**

Object Pronouns

me, you, him, her, it, them, us

94

Practice

Choose the correct pronoun. Rewrite the sentences.

Example: He smiles at _the girl_.(she/her)

He smiles at her.

1. _Horses_ are beautiful. (they/them)

2. My pet bird likes _nuts_. (they/them)

3. _Maria, Gina, and I_ like candy. (We/Us)

4. My mom talks to _my brother_. (he/him)

Apply

Talk about an animal. Use pronouns.

Example: A: Cows are big and brown.

B: They make milk for us.

Write

Tell about an animal.

Cows are big and brown. They
make milk for us. Farmers take
care of them. Cows eat grass. They
eat it all day long.

WB

39–40

Vocabulary

Words to Know

These words will help you understand the reading.

Sight Words

stay

things

place

idea

Story Words

heat

pool

cool

1. We will have to stay home and find things to do.

2. Going to Uncle Jake's place is a great idea.

3. I do not like the heat.

4. The pool is cool.

Your Turn

Pick one word from either box.

Use the word in a sentence.

Phonics

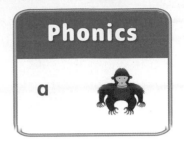
Long a

Read the words aloud. Listen for the long *a* sound.

cake

bake

snake

plate

WB PH

42

Your Turn

Sound out the words. Point to the word for the picture.

Tell if the word has a long *a* sound.

lake lock

wave wake

chick check

whale wade

97

Story Preview

Who is the play about?

Mom

Rosa

Joe

What is the play about?

**The play is about a brother and sister who
are tired of the hot weather**

Reading Strategy

Problem and Solution

A problem in a story is something that goes wrong. How
the character fixes the problem is the solution. Look for
the problem and solution as you read. Take notes.

Fun on a Hot Day

by Anya Hansen
illustrated by Gary Torrisi

Mom: Look, the sun is up. This will be another hot day.

Rosa: Not another hot day! I do not like the heat!

Joe: I don't, either. There is nothing to do when it is so hot.

Mom: It will be too hot to go outside today. We will have to stay indoors. We will find things to do at home.

Rosa: I do not want to stay home another day! I want to get out of the house.

Joe: What else can we do when it is so hot, Rosa? It's no fun to be outside in this heat.

Rosa: What about Uncle Jake? He has a pool. The water in the pool is cool. Will Uncle Jake let us swim in his pool?

Mom: That's a great idea, Rosa. I'm sure your uncle would love to have you visit.

Joe: I will call Uncle Jake to ask him if we can swim in his pool.

Mom: I bet he will invite you.

Joe: Uncle Jake invited us. We can swim in his pool!

Rosa: Hooray! We don't have to stay at home another day!

Mom: I will take you over to Uncle Jake's. You will have a wonderful time at his place.

Joe: Look, the sun is hot out there. But we are lucky. We are cool in the pool.

Rosa: If tomorrow is another hot day, I hope Uncle Jake will invite us to come swimming in his pool again!

Think It Over

 Listen to the question and say the answers.
Use Sight Words and Story Words.

1. Who are the characters in this play?

2. What problem do Rosa and Joe have?

3. How do they solve their problem?

4. What is a problem you have had? How did you solve it?

43–44

Reading Strategy

Problem and Solution

How did finding the problem and solution help you understand the play?

Grammar and Writing

Will + Verb

Use **will** + **verb** to talk about things in the future. Use **will not** for negative sentences.

> I **will have** a party tomorrow.
>
> I **will not visit** my grandparents.
>
> Tom **will watch** a parade.
>
> He **will not go** to the movies.

You can use contractions of *will*.
Change subject + **will** to subject + **'ll**.
Change **will not** to **won't**.

> I will = **I'll**
> I will not = **I won't**

To ask a question, use **will** + subject + **verb**. Use a question mark at the end of a question.

> **Will** you **go** to bed early tonight? Yes, I **will**.
>
> **Will** you **sleep** late tomorrow? No, I **won't**.

Add _will_ or _won't_. Write the sentences.

Example: <u>Will</u> you take the bus? No, I <u>won't</u>.

1. ___ it snow tomorrow? Yes, it ___.

2. ___ you go shopping? No, we ___.

3. ___ he walk the dog? Yes, he ___.

4. ___ they feed the cat? No, they ___.

 **Apply**

Ask questions about what you will do this weekend.

Example: A: Will you ride your bike?
B: Yes, I will.

Write

Tell what you will do on the weekend.

> This weekend I'll clean my room and do my chores. Then I'll go to the movies with my dad. I'll sleep late on Sunday. I will not watch TV.

WB
45–46

THE BIG Q QUESTION

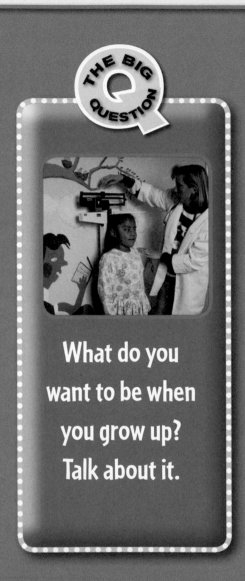

What do you want to be when you grow up? Talk about it.

Your teacher will help you choose one of these projects.

✏️ Written

Write about growing up.

How will you have changed when you grow up? What will you have learned? Write about it.

Oral

Talk about growing up.

Tell the class about what you want to be when you grow up. Why do you want to be that?

 Visual/Active

Draw yourself as a grown-up.

Draw pictures that show how you will look when you grow up.

47–48

Listening and Speaking Workshop

Interview

Conduct a formal interview with someone at school.

1 Prepare G.O. 23

Follow these directions:

1. Choose a person to interview.
2. Think about what you want to find out.
3. Make a list of questions. Use a chart like this:

Who?	Who is in your family?
Where?	Where were you born?
When?	When is your birthday?
What?	What things do you enjoy?
Why?	Why do you enjoy these activities?

2 Practice and Present

Practice your interview with a partner. Ask your partner your questions and listen to the answers. When you are ready, conduct your interview in front of the class.

110

As you speak, do this:

- Look at the person you interview.
- Speak slowly and use complete sentences.

As you listen, do this:

- Think about what you already know about this person.
- Listen for different tones of voice. They can be clues to hidden information.
- If you don't understand the speaker, ask a question.

❸ Evaluate

Ask yourself these questions:

- How well did I understand the task?
- How well did I listen? Could I summarize a classmate's interview?
- Did I understand my classmates' interviews?

> ### Listening Tip
>
> A speaker may answer a question by saying, "Of course." The expression *of course* means "yes, certainly."

111

Write to Compare and Contrast

**Compare and contrast two things that you like.
Explain how the things are alike and different.**

❶ Prewrite Choose two things to compare and contrast.
List your ideas in a graphic organizer.

Julia listed her ideas like this:

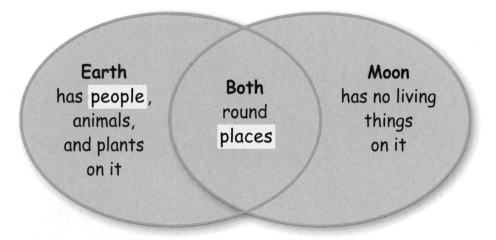

Earth
has people,
animals,
and plants
on it

Both
round
places

Moon
has no living
things
on it

❷ Draft Use your graphic organizer to help you write
a first draft. Use new words from the unit.

3 **Revise** Read your draft. Use the Revising Checklist to correct errors. Then revise your draft.

Revising Checklist

✓ Do I tell how the things are the same?

✓ Do I tell how the things are different?

✓ Are my verb tenses correct?

✓ Do my pronouns agree?

Here is Julia's work.

Julia Sanchez

The earth and the moon are both
round. ^and They are both places. But they
are not the same. The earth has
people, ^and animals, ^and on it. ~~The earth has~~
plants on it ^ ~~too~~. There are no plants
or animals on the moon. ~~The moon has~~
~~no living things on it.~~

4 **Edit** Trade papers with a partner to get feedback. Use the Editing Checklist.

5 **Publish** Make a clean copy of your final draft. Share it with the class.

Editing Checklist

✓ The sentences have different lengths and patterns.

✓ Each sentence begins with a capital letter.

✓ The sentences belong together.

Spelling Tip

Follow this rule: Add the letter *s* to many nouns to make them plural.

49–50

114

For Each Reading . . .

1. Listen to the sentences.

2. Work in pairs. Take turns reading aloud for one minute. Count the number of words you read.

> Spot is my dog. He is a puppy. I am small. Spot   12
> is small, too.   15
>   Now it is my birthday. Spot is a big dog now. I   27
> am a big kid. I am six. I have a cake and gifts.   40
> Spot and I sit and play. Spot is my best pal.   51

3. With your partner, find the words that slowed you down. Practice saying each word and then say the sentence each word is in. Then take turns reading the text again. Count the number of words you read.

WB
51–52

Unit 3

What We Like

People like different things. Tell the class about things that you like to do.

THE BIG QUESTION

What things do you like?

VIEW AND RESPOND

Watch the video. What is it about?

Talk about the poster. What does it show?

Visit LongmanCornerstone.com.

117

What Do You Know about What Children Like?

Use what you know to help you understand.

Some children like fruit.

Some children like to play outside, even when it's very cold.

Some children like to help.

Some children like sushi!

Some children like big snakes.

Your Turn

Name three things you like. Tell the class about them.

Sing about What We Like

What We Like

What we like you may not like,

ee-i-ee-i-o.

And what you like we may not like,

ee-i-ee-i-o.

I like birds and I like dogs,

ee-i-ee-i-o.

And you like pigs and you like cows,

ee-i-ee-i-o.

With a woof, woof here,

And a tweet, tweet there,

Here a moo, there an oink,

Everywhere a moo, oink.

What we like you may not like,

ee-i-ee-i-o.

Reading Tip

We read English from left to right and from top to bottom.

Antonyms and Synonyms

Antonyms are words that mean the opposite.
Synonyms are words that mean the same.

Antonyms	Synonyms
cold → hot	jump → hop
in → out	big → large

Antonyms

It is **cold** in winter.

It is **hot** in summer.

Synonyms

I go to a **big** school.

I go to a **large** school.

Your Turn

Work with a partner.
Take turns.

- Read each sentence aloud.
- Replace the underlined words with a synonym or antonym from the box.

big	now	warm	jacket

1. I like to play with my <u>little</u> brother.
2. It was so <u>hot</u>, I stopped running.
3. Where did you find my <u>coat</u>?
4. May we please talk <u>later</u>?

Vocabulary

Words to Know

These words
will help you
understand the
reading.

1. My birthday is a
   special day.
   I laugh with
   my family.

Sight Words

special

day

laugh

family

2. Today we had fun
   at the beach. We all
   played baseball.

Story Words

beach

baseball

tree

3. My friends and I
   climbed a tree.

WB

55

124

Your Turn

Pick one word from either box.

Use the word in a sentence.

Ask your teacher if you need help.

Phonics

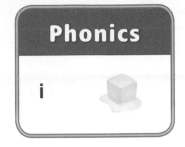
Long i

Read the words aloud. Listen for the long *i* sound.

time

kite

nine

slide

WB PH

56

Your Turn

Sound out the words. Point to the word for the picture.

Tell if it has a long *i* sound.

white   wet

file   five

smell   smile

pig   pipe

125

Story Preview

Who is in the story?

Mr. Grimes   **Jed**   **Sam**

Tim   **Tam**   **Len**

What is the story about?

The story is about fun times in families.

Reading Strategy

Author's Purpose

Authors write for different reasons, or purposes. They can make you laugh, give you information, or try to change your mind. What is the purpose of this story?

A Special Time

by Pam Walker

This is Mr. Grimes and his family. It is a special time. Mr. Grimes likes to eat and have fun with his family. Everyone laughs and has a fine time.

128

Jed and his family like to eat outside
by the lake. Jed smiles and takes a big bite.
It is a special time.

Sam's dad takes him to a baseball game.
The game is a special time. They sit in
the red seats. Dad and Sam can see it all
from there!

Sam and his dad eat snacks. Sam jumps up to get a ball. It is a special time. Sam and his dad have a lot of fun.

Tim's mom and dad take him and his
sister Val to the beach. It is a special time.

Val and Mom don't like to dig in the
sand. Val and Mom like to walk on the sand.
Waves crash behind them. It is a fine day.

Tam and her mom like to have fun on the swing. Tam and Mom swing and swing. It is a special time. Tam sings a fun song. Mom and Tam swing and clap to the song.

Len and his dad like to hike. They hike
one mile. Then they take a quick rest by
a big tree. Dad tells Len a tale that makes
him smile. It is a special time.

134

Think It Over

Audio

Listen to the questions and say the answers. Use Sight Words and Story Words.

1. What does Mr. Grimes do with his family?

2. How do Sam and his dad have a special time?

3. What is special about each time in the story?

4. How do you have a special time?

57–58

Reading Strategy

Author's Purpose

What is the author's purpose?

Grammar and Writing

Nouns

A noun is a word that names a person, place, or thing. Use **a** or **an** to talk about one noun. Use **an** before a vowel. Add **-s** to talk about two or more nouns.

It's **a tree**.
I have **an apple**.
We are at **a park**.

They are **trees**.
We have five **apples**.
I go to two **parks**.

Add **-es** to nouns ending in **-ch, -x, -s,** and **-sh**.
For nouns ending in **-y,** change the **-y** to **-ies.**

beach ⟶ beach**es**
family ⟶ famil**ies**

After one person, place, or thing, add **-s** or **-es** to a verb. For two or more, don't add **-s** or **-es**.

The boy laugh**s**. ⟶ The boys laugh.
The girl watch**es**. ⟶ The girls watch.

Reading Tip

If you don't understand, ask your teacher or a classmate for help.

Choose the correct word. Write the sentences.

Example: I have birthday (presents/present).

I have birthday presents.

1. We went to two (party/parties).

2. I see a (cake/cakes).

3. Chico (play/plays) baseball .

4. Mei Ling's friends like (balloon/balloons).

Ask and answer questions. Use nouns.

Example: A: What do you do on your birthday?

B: I have a party. We play games.

Describe what you do on your birthday.

   On my birthday, I have a party.
I have presents. I have a cake.
My family and friends come to my
party. We have fun!

59–60

Vocabulary

Audio

Words to Know

1. Who has some flowers for you? Cold water will keep them fresh.

2. A bird must roost, or rest, often.

3. Bees live in a beehive.

These words will help you understand the reading.

Sight Words

who

some

cold

keep

Story Words

roost

beehive

horse

4. My favorite animal is a horse!

Your Turn

Pick one word from either box.

Use the word in a sentence.

61

138

Phonics

Long o

Read the words aloud. Listen for the long *o* sound.

rose

hole

nose

note

62

Your Turn

Sound out the words. Point to the word for the picture.

Tell if it has a long *o* sound.

rope   rip

pot   pole

bun   bone

hill   hole

139

Story Preview

Who is in the story?

Joe

Mike and Jim

Kate

Jane

Jan

kids

Where does the story happen?

The story happens indoors.

The story happens outdoors.

Reading Strategy

Find Details

Details are bits of information. Details tell you more about the main idea. The main idea is the most important idea in the story. As you read, look for story details. Take notes.

Who Woke Up?

by Carrie Poole

illustrated by Christine Schneider

Who woke up? Joe woke up. Joe is getting an
egg from a hen. The hens are roosting in nests.
Joe is getting lots of eggs. He will keep some eggs,
and he will sell some eggs.

Who woke up? Mike and Jim woke up. The sun is up, too. Mike and Jim have eggs from Joe's farm. Mike and Jim are eating toast, too. They are having loads of fun.

Who woke up? Kate woke up. Kate is checking the bees in the beehive. Bees live close to flowers. Kate is getting honey from the beehive, and then she will take it home to eat.

Who woke up? Jane woke up. The sun is up, too. Jane is getting milk from Bell. The milk is in a pail below Bell's tummy. Jane can drink milk, and Bell can eat hay.

Who woke up? Jan woke up. Rose is up, too. Rose is a big brown horse. Jan is riding Rose in the park. Rose is trotting on the path. Rose is making Jan smile.

Cam and Ron and Sal are petting Rose on
her soft nose. Jan is glad that Rose is making
them smile.

Who woke up? Dan and Nan and Rob and Pam woke up. They are drinking cold milk. Dan is telling a joke. Nan and Rob and Pam are laughing and having a good time.

Think It Over

Audio **Listen to the questions and say the answers. Use Sight Words and Story Words.**

1. What does Joe get from the hen's nest?

2. What do Mike and Jim eat?

3. What happens in the park?

4. What do you do when you wake up?

Speaking Tip

Look at the pictures from the story again. Retell the story.

WB
63–64

Reading Strategy

Find Details

What details tell you more about what happened when Kate woke up?

Grammar and Writing

Present Progressive

Use the present progressive to talk about things that are happening now. Use **be** and add **-ing** to the main verb.

They **are making** a salad.
Dad **is chopping** carrots.
My brother **is helping**.
I **am not helping**.
I **am taking** the picture!

To add **-ing** to a word that ends in **e,** drop the **e.**

take ⟶ tak**ing**

To add **-ing** to a word that ends with a vowel and a consonant, double the consonant.

chop ⟶ chop**ping**

Reading Tip

If you don't understand, ask your teacher or a classmate for help.

Add *am, is,* or *are.* Write the sentences.

Example: Omar <u>is</u> writing.

1. Joel and Katia ___ talking.

2. I ___ listening to my teacher.

3. They ___ are standing.

4. Lan ___ getting a book.

 **Apply**

Get in a group. Talk about what the class is doing.

Example: A: Tito and Juan are talking.

      B: We are listening.

 **Write**

Describe what a classmate is doing.

Tito is sitting. He is reading. He is writing. Now he is talking to a friend. Now he is looking at me. He is waving. Hi, Tito!

Vocabulary

Audio

Words to Know

1. When we are done playing ball, we rest.

These words will help you understand the reading.

Sight Words

we

done

ball

down

2. My dad holds down the football for me. Then I can kick it.

Story Words

kick

soccer

middle

3. My friend Sarah plays soccer. She is in the middle.

WB
67

Your Turn

Pick one word from either box.

Use the word in a sentence.

Phonics

Long u

Read the words aloud. Listen for the
long *u* sound.

cube

cute

use

WB   PH

68

Your Turn

Name the pictures. Which word has the same sound as the *u* in
cube? Say the word.

t _ b

m _ le

s _ n

b _ _ s

153

Story Preview

What is the poem about?

The poem is about what kids like to do and play.

Reading Strategy

Use Prior Knowledge

Use what you know about a subject to help you
understand what you read.

Shared Reading Your teacher will show you how to use
the strategy. Listen, watch, and practice.

Playing Games

by Anya Hansen

Sports and games,
Nice folks to meet,
Fun places to visit,
And sweet treats to eat.

You can jump
And laugh and run
Into the middle of
Playing games and fun.

Up I jump
On this wonderful day,
And down I drop
On a soft pile of hay.

Up I pop
Into the warm, fresh air.
I sing and play
Without a care.

What is this game?
Here is a clue:
You kick a round ball
And run fast, too.

It's called soccer.
I bet you guessed.
This game is super;
It's the best!

I like playing soccer
It's fun in the sun.
I don't stop running
Till the game is done.

Dad holds the ball
For me to kick.
We like many sports.
Take your pick!

County fairs
Occur in June.
They are great fun
But end too soon.

We go on rides,
Eat treats by the heap,
Then say goodbye,
To get some sleep.

My name is Sue.
This game is fun.
Eighteen holes,
And I am done.

I use a club
And tap it softly.
Will it go in?
My father helps me.

Think It Over

 **Audio**

**Listen to the questions and say the answers.
Use Sight Words and Story Words.**

1. In which game do you kick a round ball?

2. How are the games alike? How are
they different?

3. What does Dad do with the football?

4. What do you like to do and play outside?

WB
69–70

Reading Strategy

Use Prior Knowledge

How did using prior knowledge help you understand what
you read?

Playing Ball

Teams

Football is a sport that needs two teams to play a game. ▶

Hoop

▲ In basketball, the ball must go through a hoop.

Bowling

The bowling ball
knocks down pins
at the end of
the lane. ▶

Baseball

▲ There are nine players
on a baseball team.

Activity to Do

These pages use pictures
and words to tell about different
ball games.

- Think of another game or
  sport that uses balls.
- Find pictures to show how
  the balls are used.
- Tell the class about
  your pictures.

165

Grammar and Writing

Adjectives

An adjective is a describing word—like **big, fun**, or **yellow**.
Adjectives describe nouns. Adjectives can go before a noun.

> It's a **special** day.
> Soccer is a **fun** game.
> That's a **big** ball.

Adjectives

bad	full	sad
dry	ill	tiny
fine	red	wet

An adjective can also follow **be**.

> The grass is **soft**.
> The sun is **warm**.
> Bubbles are **fun**.

Practice

Use adjectives to complete the sentences.

Write the sentences.

Example: It is a <u>beautiful</u> day.

1. The grass is ___.

2. It's a ___ bookcase.

3. These socks are ___.

4. The water in the pool is ___.

Apply

Describe something. Who can guess it?

Example: A: It has pictures and big words.

   B: Is it a poster?

Write

Describe an object.

I have a new soccer ball.
It's round. It's blue and white.
It can bounce. It's a good ball.

Projects

What things do you like? Describe them.

Your teacher will help you choose one of these projects.

Written

Write about a favorite outdoor place.

Where is it? What does it look like? Why do you like to go there? Write about it.

Oral

Retell a favorite story.

You probably know many stories and have read many books. Retell the story you like best.

Visual/Active

Draw a favorite activity.

Draw a picture of an activity you like to do. Talk about your picture with a friend.

73–74

Description Game

Play this game to practice describing.

1 Prepare G.O. 117

Find objects to describe. For each object, list words in a web. Here is an example for the word *pencil*.

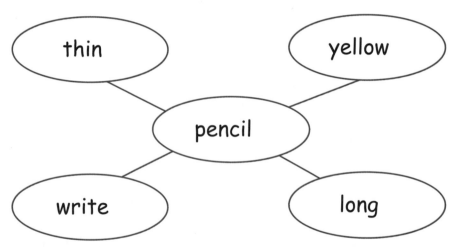

Follow your teacher's directions to play the game.

2 Practice and Present

Hide your objects. On your turn, say words that describe an object. See who can guess it. When someone guesses, hold up the object and say its name.

As you speak, do this:

- Say your words clearly.
- Have fun. Remember, this is a game.

As you listen, do this:

- Write the words in your notebook.
- Listen for words you know to help you guess the object.

3 **Evaluate**

Ask yourself these questions:

- How did the words I knew help me understand what my classmates said?
- Did I understand and follow the game rules?

More Practice

Find a picture of an object that is new to you. Don't show your partner. Describe the main points and important details of the object. Have your partner guess what it is. Then show the picture. Ask your partner to tell the most important thing about the object. Then give your partner a turn.

Writing Workshop

Write a Descriptive Paragraph

Write a paragraph telling about a birthday party that you want to have. Describe what you will see, hear, and taste at your party.

1 **Prewrite** Think about the party. List your ideas in a graphic organizer.

Mario listed his ideas in this chart.

I see...	I hear...	I taste...
the pool	my friends laughing	pizza
my friends	water splashing	birthday cake
balloons on the tables		

2 **Draft** Use your graphic organizer to help you write a first draft. Use new words from the unit.

3 **Revise** Read your draft. Use the Revising Checklist to correct errors. Then revise your draft.

Revising Checklist

✓ Do I tell about a birthday party?

✓ Do I describe sights, sounds, and tastes?

✓ Are my verb tenses correct?

✓ Do my pronouns agree?

Here is Mario's paragraph:

Mario Cueva

Next year, my party will be special. It will be at the pool. My family and my friends will c~~a~~me. We can play and swim. We can laugh and splash water. Then we can eat pizza, ~~We can eat~~ *and* yummy birthday cake. There will be balloons on the tables. The day will be fun!

4 **Edit** Trade papers with a partner to get feedback. Use the Editing Checklist.

5 **Publish** Make a clean copy of your final draft. Share it with the class.

Spelling Tip

Follow this rule: Look for smaller words inside words to help you spell correctly.

birth + day = birthday

Editing Checklist

✓ The sentences have different lengths and patterns.

✓ Each sentence begins with a capital letter.

✓ Each sentence ends with the correct mark.

✓ All the words are spelled correctly.

For Each Reading...

1. Listen to the sentences.

2. Work in pairs. Take turns reading aloud for one minute. Count the number of words you read.

This is Tim and his family. Tim's mom and dad	10
take him and his sister Val on a trip to the beach.	22
It is a special time.	27
Val and Mom don't like to dig in the sand. Val	38
and Mom like to walk on the sand. Waves crash	48
behind them. Everyone laughs and enjoys a	55
fine day.	57

3. With your partner, find the words that slowed you down. Practice saying each word and then say the sentence each word is in. Then take turns reading the text again. Count the number of words you read.

WB
77–78

Then and Now

Things are different now than in the past. Tell the class about changes in your community. How have things changed?

176

THE BIG QUESTION

How is life today different than it was a long time ago?

VIEW AND RESPOND

Watch the video. What is it about?

Talk about the poster. What does it show?

Visit LongmanCornerstone.com.

177

What Do You Know about Then and Now?

Use what you know to help you understand.

Cars today go much faster than cars from long ago.

In the past, people wrote hand-written letters to their friends. How do you write letters to your friends?

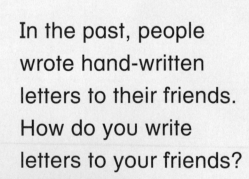

One of the games children used to play was horseshoes. What games do you like to play now?

In the past, it took a long time to travel by horse and buggy. How do you travel now?

Long ago, the best way to cook food was on a stove. How else can you cook food today?

Your Turn

If you were born before there were cars, what would you do for fun? Tell the class about it.

Sing about Then and Now

Then and Now

My grandma didn't have e-mail.

She didn't have a computer.

She just wrote letters to all of her friends

and popped them in a mailbox.

Things have changed a lot since then.

We have many inventions.

Things will change again someday,

and pop—we're in the future!

Multiple-Meaning Words

A **multiple-meaning** word has more than one meaning.

The word *last* has more than one meaning.

Pam's water will **last** through the game.

The word *last* in this sentence means Pam will have water until the end of the game.

Sam was **last** in line in the cafeteria.

The word *last* in this sentence means Sam was at the end of the line.

Rule

Reading the words and sentences around a word can help you choose the correct meaning of a multiple-meaning word.

Your Turn

Work with a partner.
Take turns.

- Read each sentence aloud.
- Choose the correct
  meaning for the underlined word.

1. That <u>kind</u> of bird is very rare.
   a. a type of something
   b. nice

2. Sue <u>lost</u> the contest.
   a. did not win
   b. could not find

3. I saw the <u>bat</u> fly through the trees.
   a. an animal that can be seen at night
   b. an object used to hit a ball

4. The feather is <u>light</u>.
   a. not weighing much
   b. an electric device

Vocabulary

Words to Know

These words
will help you
understand the
reading.

1. My friends and I cross
   two roads on our way
   to school.

2. My dad is very helpful.
   He shows me how to
   write a letter.

Sight Words

friends
roads
very
letter

3. It is simple to write
   an e-mail to our friend.

Story Words

simple
e-mail
board

4. Long ago, children
   wrote on a board
   at school. They still do.

Your Turn

Pick one word from either box.

Use the word in a sentence.

WB
81

Phonics

Long a; ch, th

Read the words aloud. Listen for the letter sounds.

pail

chick

thick   thin

spray

WB   PH
82

Your Turn

Sound out the words. Point to the word for the picture.

gray   grape

rain   rave

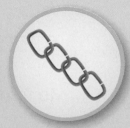

snail   snap

chain   cloth

Story Preview

What is this story about?

The story is about the past.

Reading Tip

Read on your own or with a partner.

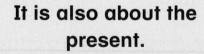

It is also about the present.

Reading Strategy

Draw Conclusions

Stories don't always tell you everything. Use story clues to form your own idea. This is how you draw a conclusion.

Times Change

by Blaze Molloy

A long time ago, we drove on roads that had a lot of rocks and bumps. A horse led the way. We used a stick and a rope to tell the horse which way to go. We pulled the rope to say, "Stop!"

We drive on safe, paved roads today. We can get home fast when we drive.

An airplane can go very fast. We can pass time on a long plane ride. Sing a long song. Play a fun game. Take a quick nap. Wake up in Spain!

This mom and dad and kids play a game called checkers. It is a simple game with just a board and game pieces. This mom and dad and kids play to win.

A bunch of kids play this game. It has bells that ring and lights that shine. The kids use electricity to play this game. A plug goes in the wall. Kids play this game to win!

This lady used a pen to write a letter. Next, she put a stamp on it. Then she put it in the mail.

We can still use stamps, but now we can send e-mails. A letter may take days to get to a friend. An e-mail is fast. It takes less than a minute to get an e-mail to a friend.

Think It Over

Listen to the questions and say the answers. Use Sight Words and Story Words.

1. How did people travel in the past?

2. What do some games need to work today?

3. What is a quicker way of sending a letter to a friend?

4. How did airplanes and e-mail change our lives?

Speaking Tip

With a partner, ask and answer questions about the story.

WB
83–84

Reading Strategy

Draw Conclusions

What conclusion did you draw?

Changing Times Audio

Locomotive ▶
These people are riding on a steam locomotive from 1845.

▲ **Passengers**
This is a bullet train in Japan. It carries passengers at very high speeds.

Television ▶

This family from the 1950s gathers around their black-and-white television.

▲ **Popular**

Wide-screen televisions are popular today.

Activity to Do

These pages use words and pictures to tell about how times have changed.

- Think of another invention that has changed the way people live.
- Find pictures of this invention and talk about them with the class.

Grammar and Writing

Simple Past Tense

Use the past tense to talk about events that happened in the past. Add **-ed** to a main verb to form the past tense.

> The friends **played** checkers
> He **laughed**.
> I **e-mailed** my sister.
> We **walked** to school.

Use **did not** or **didn't** + the base form of the verb to form the negative past tense.

> The boy **didn't laugh**.
> The team **did not play** soccer.
> Horses **didn't walk** on paved roads .

Add -ed to make the past tense. Write the sentences.

Example: Mom ___ (play) chess. Mom played chess.

1. Ken ___ (walk) to school.

2. Cam ___ (talk) with her friends.

3. We ___ (listen) to the teacher.

4. The kids ___ (use) the computer.

Get in a group. Talk about things that did not happen.

Example: A: I didn't walk to school.

   B: I didn't talk to Nina.

Write about your day.

> I walked to school. I talked
> to my friends. I listened to my
> teacher. I didn't use the computer.
> I played chess with Dad.

WB
85–86

197

Prepare to Read

These words will help you understand the reading.

Sight Words

near
good
other
sure

Story Words

tasty
treat
waffle

Vocabulary 🔊 Audio

Words to Know

1. The ice cream truck is near where we live.

2. Chocolate tastes good. How many other flavors are there? I'm not sure.

3. Ice cream is a tasty treat!

4. I love ice cream in a waffle cone.

Your Turn

Pick one word from either box.
Use the word in a sentence.

WB
87

Phonics Audio

Long e

Read the words aloud. Listen for the
long *e* sound.

tree

feet

read

me

WB   PH
88

Your Turn

Sound out the words. Point to the word for the picture.

sheep   ship   beach   back   green   grin   mat   meat

199

Story Preview

What is the story about?

The story is about ice cream.

Reading Strategy

Summarize

When you summarize, you tell only the most important ideas in a text. As you read, look for the most important ideas. Then summarize the reading.

200

On Your Own

Ice Cream Cones

by James Dubois
illustrated by Stephen Snider

Ice cream is a tasty treat. We can sit in an ice cream shop on a hot night and eat this treat. Do you like to eat ice cream?

Today, we eat ice cream in cones. But in the past, ice cream came in a dish.

A big fair was held in 1904. The sun was bright and high in the clear, blue sky. A lot of kids and adults came to play and have fun. They were hot. They ate a lot of ice cream.

An ice cream man put a scoop of ice cream in each dish. The ice cream tasted good. A lot of people ate it. The ice cream man ran out of dishes. But he had a lot of ice cream left to sell. He was not sure he could sell it all. The ice cream would melt if it didn't sell.

A **waffle** man was **near** the ice cream table. He came to help. He made a cone shape. Then the ice cream man put a scoop of ice cream in the cone. These men had made an ice cream cone!

Folks liked to eat ice cream cones at
the fair. They held ice cream cones in
their hands. Ice cream cones were fun to
eat. The kids and adults did not have
to give a dish back to the ice cream man.
Ice cream sure got easy to eat.

Kids ate ice cream cones with one another. They sat on a step and ate ice cream together. They picked the kind they liked best. Kids ate it up, and it tasted great. It is a treat a lot of kids like better than any other.

Kids still buy a lot of ice cream cones.
Kids get ice cream cones from a truck.
The trucks drive near kids' homes. When
the trucks stop, kids line up for ice cream.

Kids still eat this treat on a hot day.
It still tastes good!

Think It Over

Audio

**Listen to the questions and say the answers.
Use Sight Words and Story Words.**

1. How did people eat ice cream in the past?

2. What happened to the ice cream man's dishes?

3. How did the waffle man help the ice cream man?

4. How did the fair in 1904 change the way we eat ice cream?

WB 89–90

Reading Strategy

Summarize

How did summarizing help you understand the story?

Grammar and Writing

Past *Be*

Use the past tense of **be** to talk about the past. Use **was** with **I, he, she, it,** and one noun. Use **was not** or **wasn't** to make the negative past tense.

> The waffle **was** tasty.
> I **was** hungry.
> It **wasn't** time for lunch.
> My friend **was not** at
>   the fair.

Use **were** with **you, we, they,** and more than one noun. Use **weren't** or **were not** to make the negative past tense.

> We **were** very young.
> They **were** happy.
> The people **were not** hurt.
> You **weren't** at school yesterday.
> The children **weren't** sleepy.

Reading Tip

If you don't understand the text in the boxes, ask your teacher or a classmate for help.

Practice

Complete the sentences. Add _was_ or _were_.

Example: Pedro <u>was</u> happy.

1. The waffles ____ good.

2. The game ____ fun.

3. We ____ hungry.

4. Min-ju ____ not hurt.

Apply

Ask and answer questions about the past.

Example: A: Were you at home yesterday?

B: I wasn't at home. I was at school.

Write

Tell about your weekend.

I was at home. I was with my family. My mom and I baked cupcakes. The cupcakes were good. We were happy.

WB
91–92

211

Vocabulary Audio

Words to Know

These words will help you understand the reading.

1. Lady Bird Johnson was the wife of former President Johnson.

2. Soon after she was born, her family began calling her "Lady Bird."

3. The flowers along the highway make it look beautiful.

4. Lady Bird Johnson's legacy was the gift she left us—the idea of keeping America beautiful.

Sight Words

lady

wife

began

born

Story Words

flowers

highway

legacy

WB
93

Your Turn

Pick one word from either box.

Use the word in a sentence.

Phonics

Long i; soft g

Read the words aloud. Listen to the letter sounds.

sky

child

light

stage

WB   PH

94

Your Turn

Sound out the words. Point to the word for the picture.

page   pig

cry   crime

file   fly

note   night

213

Story Preview

What is the story about?

The story is about Lady Bird Johnson.

Reading Strategy

Ask Questions
___

Asking and answering questions as you read can help you understand the text better. Ask yourself questions as you read. Find the answers in the text.

Lady Bird Johnson

by Anya Hansen
illustrated by Daniel Mathe

Lady Bird Johnson was the wife of
President Lyndon B. Johnson. She cared a
lot about the environment and she worked
hard to preserve it.

Lady Bird Johnson was born in 1912. She was named Claudia Alta Taylor and lived in Karnack, Texas. She was said to be "as pretty as a ladybird." Her family began calling her "Lady Bird."

After college, Lady Bird met Lyndon B. Johnson. They fell in love. Soon, she became Mrs. Johnson.

In 1963, Lyndon B. Johnson became President of the United States. Lady Bird became the First Lady. She was the first first lady to have a press secretary of her own.

That was then.

While at the White House, Lady Bird gave her time to many special projects. She made the capital very beautiful by planting millions of flowers. Lady Bird also began a program to beautify highways.

And this is now.

Today Lady Bird's legacy lives on. Flowers
are still planted at the nation's capital.
Highways around the country have flowers
planted by them, too. Lady Bird worked with a
program called "Keep America Beautiful."

Lady Bird Johnson died in 2007. She was
94 years old. Lady Bird is one of the most
famous first ladies. She received many awards.
Lady Bird Johnson is remembered and loved
throughout America today.

Think It Over

Audio

**Listen to the questions and say the answers.
Use Sight Words and Story Words.**

1. How did Lady Bird get her name?

2. What things did Lady Bird Johnson do for our nation?

3. Why do you think Lady Bird was so well loved?

4. What have you done to make the environment better?

WB
95-96

Reading Strategy

Ask Questions

How did asking and answering questions while you read help you understand the text better?

Grammar and Writing

Past Tense: Irregular Verbs

Do not add **-ed** to some verbs to form the past tense. These verbs are called irregular. You have to remember the past forms of irregular verbs.

come	→	**came**
do	→	**did**
eat	→	**ate**
get	→	**got**
go	→	**went**
have	→	**had**
know	→	**knew**
leave	→	**left**
see	→	**saw**
sit	→	**sat**
stand	→	**stood**
write	→	**wrote**

Use **did not** or **didn't** + the main form of the verb to form the negative past tense of irregular verbs.

I **ate** fruit.	→	I **didn't eat** fruit.
Tim **went** to school.	→	Tim **didn't go** to school.
He **wrote** a story.	→	He **didn't write** a story.
They **sat** on the floor.	→	They **didn't sit** on the floor.

Choose the correct word. Write the sentence.

Example: She (knew/know) about flowers.
She knew about flowers.

1. He (go/went) to the store.

2. Angel (have/had) a green notebook.

3. Tasha (come/came) to the United States.

4. The Riveras (get/got) a new car.

Tell about something you did in the past.

Example: I went to Mexico. I slept at Grandma's house.

Tell about the life of someone in your family.

Grandma was born in Mexico. She had a flower store. She came to the United States. She wrote letters to her friends.

Your teacher will help you choose one of these projects.

Written

Write about school.

What was school like in the past? What is school like today? Explain.

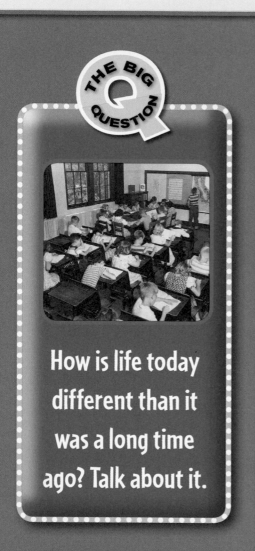

THE BIG QUESTION

How is life today different than it was a long time ago? Talk about it.

 Oral	Visual/Active
Interview an adult.	**Teach how.**
Ask an adult what school was like when he or she was your age. How did he or she learn?	Ask an adult to tell you about a game he or she used to play. Teach a partner how to play that game. Then play the game together.

Skit

Plan and act out a skit.

❶ Prepare G.O. 116

Work in groups. Three children in each group will play a
different animal. One has a problem. The other two solve
the problem. Plan your skit. List your ideas like this:

Who?	When and Where?
Diana the bird Tyler the cat Carson the squirrel	Saturday morning a tree on Mr. Yee's farm
Problem	Solution
Tyler is stuck in the tree. He can't get down.	Diana and Carson show Tyler how to get down from the tree.

Decide what props and costumes you need. Bring them in.

❷ Practice and Present
Practice the skit with your props and costumes. When
you are ready, perform your skit.

As you speak, do this:

- Pay attention to your group members so that you know when to speak.
- Use your face and body to act as your animal.

As you listen, do this:

- Look at each speaker's face and hands for clues about hidden ideas and information.
- Watch for actions and gestures you know. They will help you understand the story.

3 Evaluate

Ask yourself these questions:

- Did I perform my part of the skit well?
- How well did I listen? Which skits can I retell?

Listening Tip

Where the action of the skit "takes place" is where and when it happens. The expression *take place* means to happen.

Writing Workshop

Write a Story

Write a story. Create some characters and tell what happens to them.

1 **Prewrite** Think about your story. List your ideas for the story in a graphic organizer.

Lee listed his ideas in this graphic organizer.

Who is in the story?	Where does it happen?
Jack, a dog Jack's owner, Milo Sally, a cat	in a neighborhood
What is the problem?	**How is it solved?**
Jack chased Sally and got lost.	Sally showed Jack how to get home.

2 **Draft** Use your graphic organizer to help you write a first draft. Use new words from the unit.

3 Revise Read your draft. Use the Revising Checklist to correct errors. Then revise your draft.

Revising Checklist

✓ Do I tell what happens to the characters?

✓ Do my subjects and verbs agree?

✓ Do I use the connecting word *and* correctly?

Here is Lee's story.

Lee Ortiz

Jack the Dog

Milo took Jack for a walk. Jack saw Sally. Jack pulled his leash out of Milo's hand and chased Sally down the road. He ~~cannot~~ could not catch her. When Jack stopped, he was ~~not near home~~ lost. Sally walked Jack home. "You sure are a good friend," he told her. He wagged his tail. Jack never chased cats again.

4 **Edit** Trade papers with a partner to get feedback. Use the Editing Checklist.

5 **Publish** Make a clean copy of your final draft. Share it with the class.

Editing Checklist

✓ The sentences have different lengths and patterns.

✓ Regular and irregular verbs are used correctly.

✓ The possessive case (apostrophe **-s**) is used correctly.

Spelling Tip

For words with the CVC pattern, such as *wag*, double the consonant before adding *-ed*.

For Each Reading...

1. Listen to the sentences.

2. Work in pairs. Take turns reading aloud for one minute. Count the number of words you read.

While at the White House, Lady Bird Johnson	8
made the capital beautiful by planting flowers.	15
She also began a program to beautify highways.	23
Today Lady Bird's legacy lives on. Flowers are	31
still planted at the nation's capital. Highways	38
have flowers, too. We think of her when we see	48
the words "Keep America Beautiful."	53

3. With your partner, find the words that slowed you down. Practice saying each word and then say the sentence each word is in. Then take turns reading the text again. Count the number of words you read.

WB
103–104

Plants and Animals

Plants and animals are important in our world. Tell the class about plants and animals where you live.

THE BIG QUESTION

Why are plants and animals important in our world?

VIEW AND RESPOND

Watch the video. What is it about?

Talk about the poster. What does it show?

Visit LongmanCornerstone.com.

What Do You Know about Plants and Animals?

Use what you know to help you understand.

Some animals help us.

We can use some plants as food.

We need animals and plants so we can live.

We can take care of plants.

We can take care of animals.

Your Turn

What is your favorite animal? Why? Tell the class about it.

Sing about Plants and Animals 🎧

In Our World

Cats and birds and fish and dogs,
they are animals in our world.
Fleas and flies, elephants, too,
whales and turtles and kangaroos,
cats and birds and fish and dogs,
they are animals in our world.

Daisies, roses, and palm trees—
plants that make our planet green.
Bushes of blueberries, and lemon trees,
pines and ferns and strawberries,
daisies, roses, and palm trees—
plants that make our planet green.

Word Study

Prefixes

A **prefix** is a word part added to the beginning of a word. A prefix changes the meaning of the word.

Prefixes can help you understand new words.

unhappy = un + happy   retell = re + tell

Rule

The prefix *un-* means "not." So ***unhappy*** means "not happy."

The prefix *re-* means "again." So ***retell*** means "to tell again."

Your Turn

**Work with a partner.
Take turns.**

- Read each pair of sentences aloud.

- Complete the second sentence. Add the prefix *un-* or *re-* to the underlined word. Sound out the new word.

    1. My team was <u>lucky</u> to win the game.
       My team was ＿＿ today and lost the game.

    2. We can <u>use</u> this bottle to carry water.
       We can ＿＿ this bottle to carry water.

    3. I <u>painted</u> my bedroom a light green.
       I ＿＿ my bedroom a dark green.

    4. My friend told me a story that was <u>true</u>. My friend told me a story that was ＿＿.

    5. I try to eat <u>healthy</u> foods.
       I avoid ＿＿ foods.

Vocabulary Audio

Words to Know

These words
will help you
understand the
reading.

1. I have a small ball. I found
   the ball at the beach.

Sight Words

have

small

found

2. The squirrel
   nibbles on a nut.

3. It's delicious!

Story Words

squirrel

nibbles

delicious

Your Turn

Pick one word from either box.

Use the word in a sentence.

Work with a partner.

WB
107

Phonics

Long o; soft g

Read the words aloud. Listen for the letter sounds.

soap

gem

snow

cold

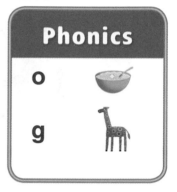

Phonics

o

g

WB PH
108

Your Turn

Sound out the words. Point to the word for the picture.

boat   bite

gull   goal

stop   stage

got   goat

243

Story Preview

Who is in the story?

bird

spider

squirrel

Where does the story happen?

The story happens in trees.

Reading Tip

Read on your own or with a group.

Reading Strategy

Cause and Effect

A cause is why something happens. An effect is what happens as a result of a cause. Look for causes and effects as you read.

What Lives in a Tree?

by Sonia Black

A nest with eggs sits high in this tree.
Twigs, twine, and trash make up this
nest. Mother bird will wait till her chicks
grow in the eggs. Small chicks will poke
holes and crack the shells. Then Mother
will find a meal her chicks can eat.

A spider spins a sticky web high in an oak tree. When it has finished, it will hide and wait for an insect. An insect will fly by and get stuck in the web. Then our spider pal can have a fine meal to eat.

Some squirrels roam around and make homes in trees. They hunt and find nuts that lie on the ground. They crack nuts with sharp teeth.

This squirrel nibbles on a tasty snack he found. He eats his nut on a leaf pile.

Squirrels jump from homes in trees and try to find a lot of nuts. They dig in leaf piles to find nuts. They find loads and loads of nuts and pile them up at home. They keep the nuts at home to eat when it is cold outside.

We don't live in trees. But trees provide things we need to live.

We get foods such as nuts and berries from trees. Books that kids read are made from trees. A tree gave us this book.

Trees help give us air. Trees help us get the clean air we need to breathe.

And trees can help us make the homes we go to each night.

Think It Over

Audio **Listen to the questions and say the answers. Use Sight Words and Story Words.**

1. What animal makes a nest in the tree?

2. What will get stuck in the spider's web?

3. What can we get from trees?

4. Why are trees important?

109–110

Reading Strategy

Cause and Effect

Name some causes and effects you found in the story.

251

Trees

Bloom ▶

This is a cherry tree in full bloom. In the summer, people will pick red cherries.

◀ **Ripe**

Soon, someone will pick this ripe peach.

Furniture ▶

This tree is called a sycamore maple. People make furniture from this kind of tree.

▲ Almond

Almonds grow on this tree.

Activity to Do

These two pages tell about different trees.

- Think of a few ways that people use trees.
- Find pictures that show some ways trees are used.
- Talk about your pictures with the class.

253

Grammar and Writing

Prepositions of Location

In, *on*, *at*, *next to*, *under*, and *between* are prepositions of location. They tell the location of places and things.

> **on** the floor
> **in** the room
> **at** the school
> **next to** the blackboard
> **under** the table
> **between** the desks

Use prepositions of location to answer questions with *where*.

> Where is the poster?
> It's **on** the wall.

> Where is the chair?
> It's **next to** the desk.

254

Practice

Add prepositions to complete the sentences.

Example: The books are __on__ the shelf.

1. My feet are ____ the desk.

2. The bed is ____ the table.

3. The picture is ____ the wall.

4. It's ____ the TV and the window.

Apply

Talk about a room. Use prepositions of location.

Example: A: Where is the rug?

                 B: It's on the floor.

Write

Describe a room in your home.

    The bed is next to the window.
The table is between the wall and
the bed. The pictures are on the
wall. The toys are under the bed.

WB
111–112

Vocabulary

Words to Know

These words will help you understand the reading.

1. Mom **was** sitting with me. I **said** to her, "Let's go out **soon**, while it's sunny." Mom said, "Ok. I'll bring some **water** for us to drink."

Sight Words

was

said

soon

water

2. You have to have strong **arms** to row a boat! We like to stay close to **shore**.

Story Words

arms

shore

sign

3. The **sign** is pointing straight ahead to the panda habitat.

WB

113

Your Turn

Pick one word from either box.
Use the word in a sentence.

Phonics

Letters: ew, ou

Phonics

moon

Read the words aloud. Listen for the letter sounds.

soup

screw

new

WB PH
114

Your Turn

Name the pictures. Which words have the same sound as the *ew* in *new*? Say the words.

257

Story Preview

Who is in the story?

Sue

Dad

Mom

Where does the story happen?

The story happens in a pond.

Reading Strategy

Sequence of Events

The sequence of events is the order in which things happen in a story. Look for the sequence of events as you read.

Sue the Tadpole

by Quentin Shue
illustrated by Kevin Rechin

Sue, the new tadpole, rested on a
leaf. She rested on a leaf in the deep blue
water. Dad and Mom saw Sue. The bugs
saw Sue. A fish saw Sue. A bird flew by.
Sue felt alone. Sue felt a bit scared.

Mom held Sue gently. Sue was cold
and wet. She moaned, "Mom, when
will I be a big frog?"

Mom said, "Soon. It is true. You
will be a big frog in a few weeks."

Sue swam in the pond. She said sadly,
"I have no arms or legs. I can dive. I can
swim. But I cannot jump. I want to be a
real frog."

Sue saw Dad jump and hop. Dad jumped from leaf to leaf. Sue was still sad.

"When will I grow up to be a real frog?" she asked.

"Soon," Dad said. "You will be a big frog in a few weeks."

Sue was getting bigger. She had a tail.
But where were her arms and legs? A
fish swam by. The fish stopped to chat
with Sue.

Sue was tired. She moaned, "I have a tail now, but I have no arms or legs. I want to be a real frog." Sue wished for arms and legs so she could jump like her dad.

265

Time went by slowly. Sue swam
in the deep blue water. Her legs were
growing. She swam fast. She still wanted
to be big enough to swim with her dad.

Time went by. Sue's legs grew and grew. New arms were growing, too. Sue could not wait to jump just like her dad.

Sue was excited. She said to Dad,
"Look at me. I can jump. I can hop.
Mom said I would get big. She said
I would grow. Mom was right, and I
am glad! Yippee!"

Dad and Sue sat on a lily pad. They
saw their faces in the deep blue water.
Sue and Dad smiled. They were so happy.
Sue was a real frog now. She could hop, and
she could jump. Sue wanted to hop and
jump all the time.

Sue read a sign on the shore. There
was a jumping show.

Sue was a good jumper now. She won
the show. Sue got a prize. Sue thought,
"Waiting for arms and legs was hard, but
they were worth waiting for!"

Think It Over

Audio

Listen to the questions and say the answers. Use Sight Words and Story Words.

1. What problem does Sue have?

2. How do Mom and Dad help Sue?

3. What does Sue learn at the end of the story?

4. How do tadpoles change as they grow?

Speaking Tip

Look at the pictures from the story again. Retell the story.

WB
115–116

Reading Strategy

Sequence of Events

How did thinking about the sequence of events help you understand the story?

Grammar and Writing

Adverbs of Manner

An adverb describes the action of a verb. Add **-ly** to an adjective to make some adverbs.

The cat moves **quietly**.
The bird sings **beautifully**.
The sun shines **brightly**.

Well is the adverb form of **good**.

Julia writes **well**.
This dog does not swim **well**.

Use adverbs to complete the sentences.

Example: She talked <u>quietly</u> (quiet).

1. The lonely dog moaned ____ (sad).

2. Frogs have strong legs. They jump very ____ (good).

3. The bees buzzed ____ (loud). They made lots of noise.

4. The sun set ____ (slow).

Use adverbs to describe what the class is doing.

Example: A: Sandra and Juan are reading quietly.

B: Daniela is listening carefully.

Write

Describe how an animal moves.

> The cat sits quietly. It watches the bird carefully. Suddenly, it jumps up. It does not catch the bird. The cat slowly walks away.

WB
117–118

273

Reading 3

Prepare to Read

Vocabulary

Words to Know

These words will help you understand the reading.

Sight Words

ground
air
more
animals

Story Words

ocelot
river
ecosystem

1. Water, the ground, and the air are each part of an ecosystem.

2. An ecosystem is more than just the plants and animals that live in it.

3. A desert is an ecosystem. There are many animals that live in the desert. One example is the ocelot.

4. If a river flows through or close to a desert, the land near the river can be very different from the desert. It is part of an ecosystem.

Your Turn

Pick one word from either box.

Use the word in a sentence.

Phonics

Letters: ow, ou

Read the words aloud. Listen for the letter sounds.

loud

town

WB PH
120

Your Turn

Which letters are missing?

__ l   cl _ _ d   cr _ _ n   m _ _ se

275

Story Preview

What is the story about?

ecosystems

the desert

plants

animals

Where does the story happen?

The story happens in the desert.

Reading Strategy

Make Inferences

Sometimes text includes ideas that are not directly stated. When you make inferences, you use clues from the text to help you understand these ideas.

Ecosystems, Plants, and Animals

by Anya Hansen

The United States is so big that it has many different ecosystems. An ecosystem is a place where different plants and animals live. But an ecosystem is more than just the plants and animals that live in it. Things like mountains, climate, bodies of water, the ground, and the air are also part of the ecosystem.

One ecosystem in the United States is called the desert. In the desert, the land is dry.

The plants that grow there can live without much water. Most of these plants are grasses and low bushes. Some have sharp pieces, like thorns, that help keep the plants safe from animals.

One animal that lives in the desert is a wild cat called an ocelot. The ocelot is about twice as big as a pet cat and has fur with lots of spots. The spots help the ocelot to hide so it can be safe and look for food. Ocelots come out at night. They may hunt birds, fish, and other small animals.

Sadly, there are very few ocelots in deserts today. Because of all of the new cities and towns, the ocelot's habitat is getting smaller. Today, ocelots do not have many places to live.

If a river flows through or close to a desert, the land near the river can be very different. Where the river flows, the land and the air are not dry. Different plants can grow in this place. Many different trees that need lots of water grow around rivers that flow through or close to deserts.

Many different birds live around the river. Some of them live there year round. But others do not always live there. They come from other places. They stay for a short time and then fly back home.

The desert is just one of the ecosystems in the United States. Do you want to know about the ecosystems around your home?

Think It Over

Audio

**Listen to the questions and say the answers.
Use Sight Words and Story Words.**

1. What is an ecosystem?

2. Why are there so many ecosystems in the United States?

3. Why are there so few ocelots in deserts today?

4. If you could visit the desert, what would you want to see?

WB
121–122

Reading Strategy

Make Inferences

How did making inferences help you understand the story?

Grammar and Writing

Possessives and Possessive Pronouns

Use the possessive form to show that someone owns something. Use **'s** to make the possessive form of the noun. To make the possessive form for more than one noun, add **'** after the **s**.

Mom**'s** car is
    blue.
That is my
    friend**'s** ball.

My parent**s'** car
    is blue.
That is my
    friend**s'** ball.

Use a possessive adjective in front of a noun to show possession. Use a possessive pronoun in place of a noun.

It is **my** book.	→	It is **mine**.
It is **your** ball.	→	It is **yours**.
It is **her** pen.	→	It is **hers**.
It is **our** house.	→	It is **ours**.
It is **their** car.	→	It is **theirs**.

Make the possessive form. Write the sentences.

Example: It is (Diego) paper. It is Diego's paper.

1. It is the (teachers) room.

2. They are the (students) notebooks.

3. The red box is (Sofia).

4. I have my (mother) bag.

Describe things that are yours.

Example: A: My notebook is red.

              B: The red notebook is yours.

Describe something you own.

> My bike is green. It has a white stripe. It has a bell and a basket. It has reflectors that keep me safe. My bike is new. It's my favorite thing.

WB
123–124

Your teacher will help you choose one of these projects.

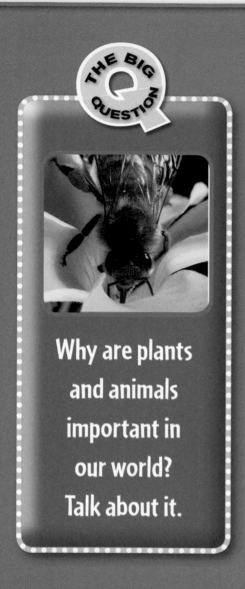

THE BIG QUESTION

Why are plants and animals important in our world? Talk about it.

✏ Written

Write about your favorite animal.

What does it look like?
What do you like most about it? Describe it.

Oral	**Visual/Active**
Describe a plant or an animal.	**Draw your favorite plant or animal.**
Describe for the class a plant or an animal from another country.	Draw a picture of your favorite plant or animal.

WB
125–126

Speech

Prepare and give a formal speech.

1 Prepare G.O. 109

Think about something you like or dislike. Explain your reasons for liking or disliking this thing. List your ideas in a chart like this:

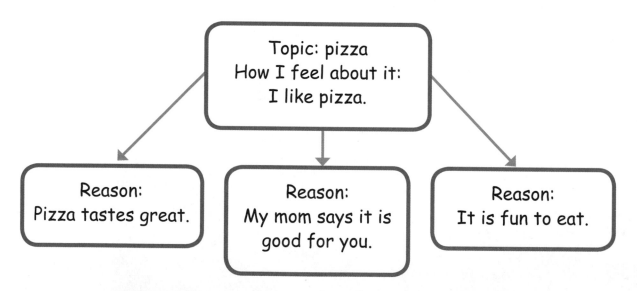

Topic: pizza
How I feel about it:
I like pizza.

Reason:
Pizza tastes great.

Reason:
My mom says it is good for you.

Reason:
It is fun to eat.

Think about pictures or props you can use during your speech.

2 Practice and Present

Practice your speech in front of a mirror. Practice speaking with expression. Try not to use your notes. Then give your speech in front of the class. Use pictures or props during your speech.

As you speak, do this:

- Use sentences of different lengths and types.
- Use connecting words such as *and, but,* and *or.*
- Speak slowly and use complete sentences.

As you listen, do this:

- Notice pauses. A pause could be a clue to a hidden idea.
- Take notes. If you don't understand something, write a question. Ask it afterwards.
- Look at the visuals to help you understand the speaker.

❸ Evaluate

Ask yourself these questions:

- Did my audience hear me clearly?
- Did I understand my classmates' speeches?

More Practice

Work with a partner. Choose a topic that is new to both of you. Find out some facts about the topic. Then give a talk about what you learned. Tell your partner the main points and most important details. Ask your partner to tell the general meaning of your talk. Then switch roles.

Write a Description

Write a paragraph describing a place you know well. Tell about what you see, hear, smell, and feel at this place.

1 **Prewrite** Think about a place that is special to you. Think about how it looks, sounds, smells, and feels. List your ideas in a graphic organizer.

Bing listed her ideas in this graphic organizer.

I see . . .	I hear . . .	I smell . . .	I feel . . .
white sand	waves crashing	salt water	warm sand
foamy waves	sea gulls screaming	hot dogs	cool water

2 **Draft** Use your graphic organizer to help you write a first draft. Use new words from the unit.

3 Revise Read your draft.
Use the Revising Checklist
to correct errors. Then revise
your draft.

Here is Bing's description:

Bing Chu

The Beach

The beach is special. The white
sand is warm. Sometimes it is to° hot.
Then I jump in to the water. The
water feels cool, and The air smells salty.
I watch the waves crash on the shore.
I like that sound. The sea gulls
scream. They want the delicious hot
dogs. I give them a small bite.

4 **Edit** Trade papers with a partner to get feedback. Use the Editing Checklist.

5 **Publish** Make a clean copy of your final draft. Share it with the class.

Editing Checklist

✓ The sentences flow smoothly.

✓ The verb tenses are correct.

✓ All words are spelled correctly.

Spelling Tip

The long *e* sound can be spelled with these patterns: *ee* as in *feel* or *ea* as in *beach*.

For Each Reading...

I. Listen to the sentences.

2. Work in pairs. Take turns reading aloud for one minute. Count the number of words you read.

Squirrels roam around and make homes in	7
trees. They hunt and find nuts that lie on the	17
ground. They crack nuts with sharp teeth.	24
Squirrels try to find a lot of nuts. They dig in	35
leaf piles to find nuts. They find loads and loads	45
of nuts and pile them up at home. They keep the	56
nuts at home to eat when it is cold outside.	66

3. With your partner, find the words that slowed you down. Practice saying each word and then say the sentence each word is in. Then take turns reading the text again. Count the number of words you read.

WB
129–130

Unit 6

Different Places

People in different places have different cultures and languages. Tell the class about other countries you know.

VIEW AND RESPOND

Watch the video. What is it about?

Talk about the poster. What does it show?

Visit LongmanCornerstone.com.

What Do You Know about Different Places?

Use what you know to help you understand.

In some countries, brides wear a red dress.

In some countries, brides wear a white dress.

296

Some people use chopsticks to eat.

In parts of the world, people use forks and knives to eat.

Some people do not use cars to travel. They travel by camel.

Your Turn

Have you seen more pictures of people in other countries? How were they different from you? Tell the class about it.

297

Sing about Different Places

Many Cultures, Many Ways

All around the world,
   people come and go.
They live in little houses,
   tall buildings, farms, and more.
They dress in thick, warm coats,
   in turbans, and light shirts.
There are many, many cultures,
   and many, many ways.

Some kids walk to school,
   some kids go by car.
Others go by bike,
   or on a camel's back.
They all will study hard,
   and soon they will learn
   there are many, many countries,
   and many, many ways.

Word Study

Suffixes

A **suffix** is a word part added to the end of a word. A suffix changes the meaning of the word. Suffixes can help you understand new words.

rainy = rain + y   slowly = slow + ly

Rule

The suffix -*y* means "full of." So ***rainy*** means "full of rain."

The suffix -*ly* means "in a certain way." So ***slowly*** means "in a slow way."

Your Turn

**Work with a partner.
Take turns.**

- Read each pair of sentences aloud.

- Say the underlined word.

- Add *-y* or *-ly* to the underlined word and sound it out. Read the completed sentence aloud.

1. The beach is full of <u>sand</u>.
   The beach is ____.

2. The dog moved in a <u>quick</u> way.
   The dog moved ____.

3. Her hair was combed in a <u>neat</u> way.
   Her hair was ____ combed.

4. The sea is full of <u>salt</u>.
   The sea is ____.

Vocabulary

Audio

Words to Know

These words will help you understand the reading.

Sight Words

around

world

warm

Story Words

vegetables

cabbage

tofu

1. We want to go around the world to a warm place!

2. There are many kinds of vegetables. A cabbage is a vegetable.

3. Eating tofu is good for you.

Your Turn

Pick one word from either box.

Use the word in a sentence. Work with a partner.

Phonics

R controlled vowels: ir, er, ur

Read the words aloud. Listen for the letter sounds.

girl

sunburn

winter

shirt

Phonics

bird

nurse

fern

WB PH

134

Your Turn

Sound out the words. Point to the correct word. Write the words.

bed bird

skirt skit

cold curl

summer smell

Story Preview

Who is in the story?

Bayo

Lee

Tori

Reading Tip

Read on your own or with your teacher.

Where does the story happen?

Nigeria

Ireland

Japan

Reading Strategy

Use Visuals

Maps, photographs, and other visuals contain information. This information helps you understand the text. Look at the visuals as you read the story.

Pen Pals

by Jeff Cole

Africa

Nigeria

Dear Pen Pal,

My name is Bayo. My home is in Nigeria. It is hot and dry there.

I like to eat warm bread with meat and rice. Yams, soups, and stews are things I eat, too.

I like to play tag with my friends. I chase them, and I run as fast as I can.

I think we can make friends with each other. I hope you send me a note.

Bayo

Ireland

Europe

Dear Pen Pal,

My name is Lee. Ireland is my home. It is not hot and dry. It is a bit wet.

I like to eat a meal with cabbage and meat. Mom cooks it in a big pot. I eat out of a bowl.

My dog, Big Skip, and I can herd sheep. Big Skip can run around them. This keeps them together.

I want to find out about you and your world. It will be fun.

Lee

307

Dear Pen Pal,

My name is Tori. That name means "bird" in my home, Japan.

I like to eat vegetables, tofu, fish, and rice. On warm days, I like to fly my big red kite. It is fun.

I hope you send a note. First I will read it. Then I will send a note back.

I want to know about your world. We can be pen pals.

Tori

Think It Over

Audio **Listen to the questions and say the answers. Use Sight Words and Story Words.**

1. Where does Bayo live?

2. What job does Big Skip have?

3. Look at Japan on the map. Why do people there eat a lot of fish?

4. Why do you think people from different places eat such different foods?

Speaking Tip

If you don't understand something about the story, ask a partner a question.

WB
135–136

Reading Strategy

Use Visuals

How did using visuals help you understand the reading?

Grammar and Writing

Capitalization

Use capitals for proper nouns. Proper nouns are names of people, places and things.

> Kids eat tofu in **J**apan.
> We went to **H**ermann **P**ark.
>
> I live on **A**rapaho **S**treet.
> My teacher is **M**s. **M**itchell.

Use capitals for names of days of the week, months, and holidays. Do not use capitals for the names of the seasons.

> It's **W**ednesday.
> My birthday is in **A**pril.
> We don't go to school on
> **L**abor **D**ay.
> It is warm in **N**ew **Y**ork in
> the summer.

2010   **April**

SUN	MON	TUE	WED	THU	FRI	SAT
				1	2	3
4	5	6	7	8	9	10
11	12	13	14	15	16	17
18	19	20	21	22	23	24
25	26	27	28	29	30	

Use capitals in the greetings and closings of letters.

> **D**ear **M**arisa,
> **D**ear **M**r. **S**mith,
>
> **Y**our friend, **H**ilda
> **S**incerely, **D**aniel **G**arcia

Choose the correct word. Write the sentences.

Example: It's <u>spring</u> (Spring/spring).

1. In _____ (nigeria/Nigeria), kids play tag.

2. I like to fly kites with _____ (tori/Tori).

3. They speak Spanish in _____ (Mexico/mexico).

4. There are tall mountains in _____ (Peru/peru).

Get in a group. Talk about places you like.

Example: A: I have fun playing at Hermann Park.

B: I like to eat at Pizza Palace.

Write about a country.

> Spain is a country in Europe. The
> people speak Spanish. There are
> old buildings. The people eat Tapas.

137–138

Prepare
to Read

Vocabulary

Words to Know

These words
will help you
understand the
reading.

1. It's raining! It would
   be better to wait
   before I go outside.

Sight Words

would

better

only

under

2. Only two kids fit
   under this
   umbrella.

Story Words

students

continent

3. The third-grade
   students in my
   school study
   geography.

4. We live on the
   continent of
   North America.

Your Turn

Pick one word from either box.

Use the word in a sentence.

139

312

Phonics

R controlled vowel: ar

Read the words aloud. Listen for the letter sounds.

 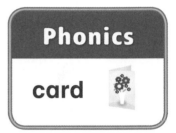

stars

park

jar

shark

140

Your Turn

Name the pictures. Which words have the same sound as the *ar* in *card*? Say the words. Write the words.

Story Preview

What is the story about?

schools

Where does this story happen?

**The story happens in different places
around the world.**

Reading Strategy

Main Idea and Details

The main idea is the most important idea in a story.
Details support, or add information to, the main idea. As
you read, look for the main idea and details. Take notes.

Schools Around the World

You are here.

by Skip Flag

This class would like to learn
more about students around the
world. Pictures and maps will help
this class find out more.

This class can also read notes
from students in other lands.
They will enjoy getting lots of
letters from kids in other places.

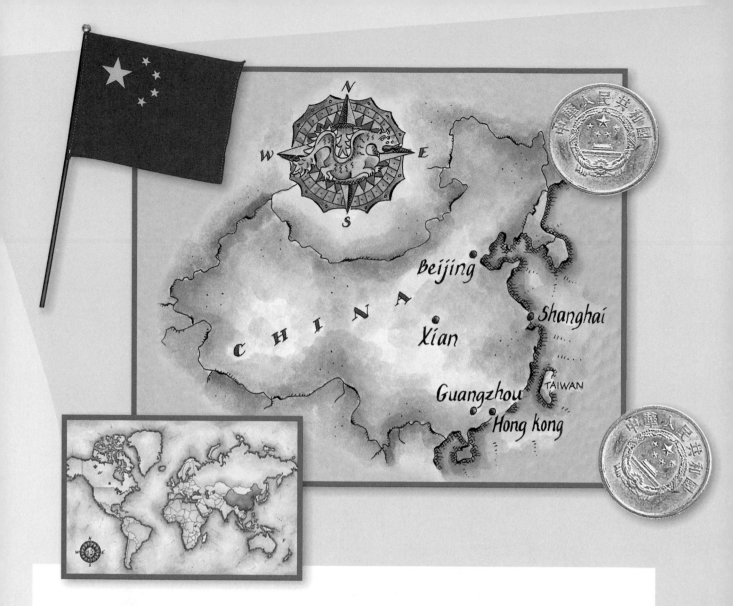

Dear Class,

I live on a big continent. It is called Asia. I live in a country called China.

My flag has only two colors. It is red with yellow stars. One star is big. The other stars are not big. I would like to see your flag.

I want to be a better student. I work hard for my teacher. I stand up and read in class.

When it is time for lunch, I eat with girls and boys in my class. When I go home, I help my mom and dad. Then I go to sleep.

Chun

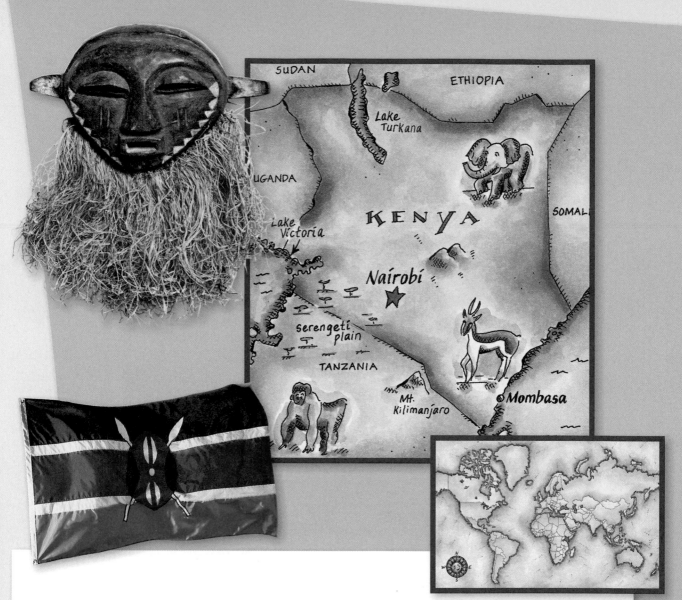

Dear Class,

I live in Kenya. This is my flag. It is black and red and green. It has white stripes.

It is hot in my country. My home is close to the sea. When it is hot, I jump in the sea. I dive under the waves.

My school is lots of fun. I like to read and sing and dance in class. When it is time for lunch, I eat under a big tree in the yard.

At home, I have chores to do. I like my schoolwork better than my chores.

Ande

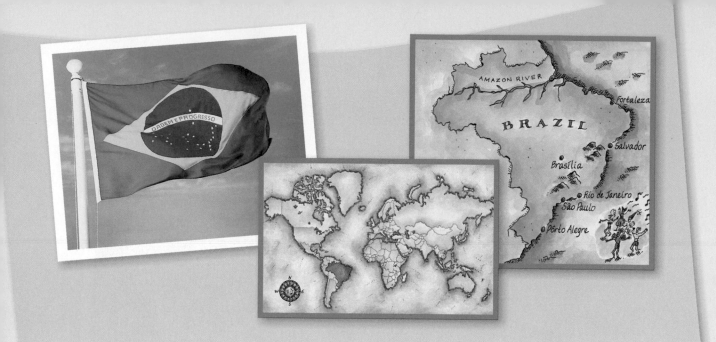

Dear Class,

I was born in Brazil. This is my flag. Green is for land and blue is for sea. Yellow is for the sun that shines each day. The sun helps palm trees grow in my country.

My home is by the shore. I play in warm sand.

I would like to learn more about your home. Please send me a letter to help me learn.

Marco

Think It Over

Audio **Listen to the questions and say the answers.
Use Sight Words and Story Words.**

1. Where is Chun from?

2. Give two details about Ande.

3. How are these children's lives like yours?

4. How would you answer Marco's letter?

141–142

Reading Strategy

Main Idea and Details

How did finding the main idea and details help you understand
the reading?

Schoolchildren Around the World

Audio

Chicago ▶

These students go to school in Chicago, Illinois, USA.

▲ **South Africa**

Former President Clinton meets schoolchildren in South Africa.

Russia ▶

These Russian schoolchildren walk to school through the snow.

▲ **China**

Some Chinese schoolchildren wear uniforms like the ones shown here.

Activity to Do

These two pages use pictures and words to tell about schoolchildren around the world.

- Think about how schoolchildren from around the world are alike. How are they different?
- Find pictures that show other schoolchildren.
- Tell the class about your pictures.

Grammar and Writing

Infinitive

Use the infinitive to talk about a verb without time. Use *to* + the main verb. Use the infinitive with *like to*, *want to,* and *would like to*.

Joel **would like to go** to Kenya.

They **want to eat** treats.

I **want to be** a better student.

Ande **likes to sing**.

Use *don't/doesn't like to* or *don't/doesn't want to* to make the negative infinitive.

I **don't want to go** under the waves.

He **doesn't like to do** his chores.

326

Add the infinitive. Write the sentences.

Example: Eru likes (sing) <u>to sing</u>.

1. Mai wants (walk) ___ to the park.

2. I would like (listen) ___ to my favorite song.

3. They would like (be) ___ good students.

4. Kim likes (dance) ___.

Talk about what you want to do when you grow up.

Example: A: What do you want to be when you grow up?

B: I would like to be a pilot.

Write about what you want to do when you grow up.

> Max wants to be a pilot. He wants to fly a plane. I want to be a sheep farmer. I would like to have a sheep dog.

143–144

These words
will help you
understand the
reading.

Sight Words

morning
once
work
school

Story Words

moment
different
country

Vocabulary

Words to Know

1. It's Monday morning.
   Once I get up, I will
   eat breakfast.

2. We work hard
   in school!

3. Let's look at this
   map for a moment.
   What different
   countries do you see?

4. This is Greenland. It
   is a part of a country
   called Denmark.

Your Turn

Pick one word from either box.

Use the word in a sentence.

145

Phonics

R controlled vowels: or, ore

Read the words aloud. Listen for the letter sounds.

storm

fork

shore

Phonics

horn

store

WB PH

146

Your Turn

Name the pictures. Which words have the same sound as the *or* in *horn*? Say the words. Write the words.

329

Story Preview

Who is in the story?

Mark

Star

Carl

Jane

Ned

Dar

Where and at what time does this story happen?

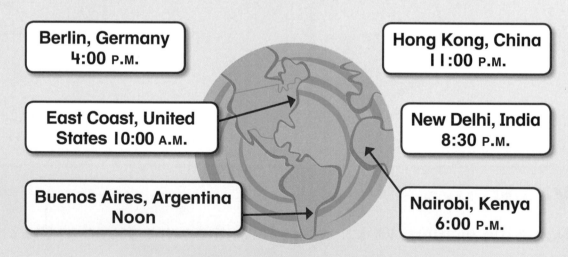

Berlin, Germany
4:00 P.M.

Hong Kong, China
11:00 P.M.

East Coast, United
States 10:00 A.M.

New Delhi, India
8:30 P.M.

Buenos Aires, Argentina
Noon

Nairobi, Kenya
6:00 P.M.

Reading Strategy

Make Connections

Making connections as you read can help you see how ideas are related. Doing this can help you understand the text better.

Time at School and at Home

by Sam Page

My name is Mark.

This morning I will find out about kids from different lands. I will use this globe to show me where their homes are.

Then I will read a book to learn about kids in other lands. It will be fun to read and find out new facts.

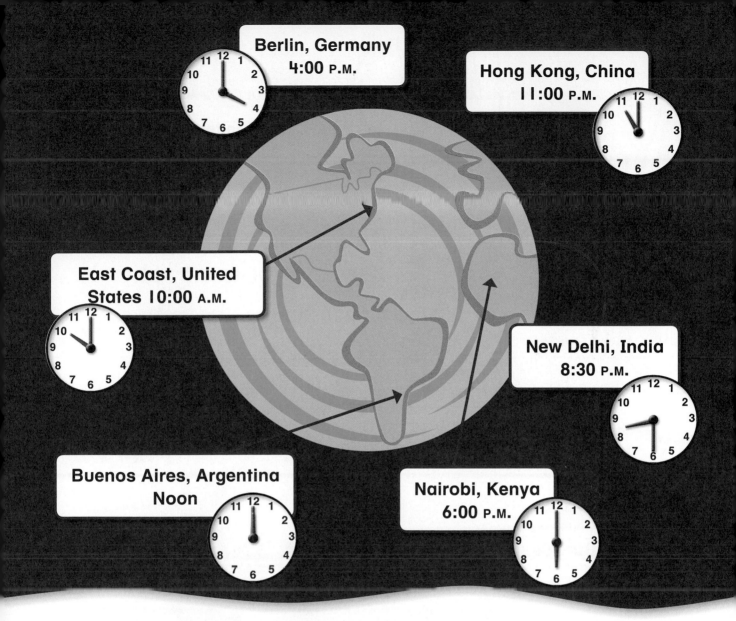

Green means land on this globe and blue means water. I will send a note to girls and boys in each country .

I will ask them to tell me about their lives. I can ask how boys and girls go to school. Then I can learn what games they play.

West Coast, United States
9:00 A.M.

This is Star. In the morning, Star reads in her classroom at school. Star likes to share her books with her friends.

Buenos Aires, Argentina
2:00 P.M.

This is Carl. Carl likes to eat lunch with his friends. Carl has fun throughout the day.

Berlin, Germany
4:00 P.M.

This is Jane and her dad. After school, Jane and her dad visit a big park. They will go home when it gets dark outside.

Nairobi, Kenya
6:00 P.M.

These boys like to play soccer after school. Once their team won a big game. Today, Jim, Sam, and Ned will teach other kids how to play.

335

This is Hana. Hana will do her work when she gets home. Then she will tell her mom and dad about her day.

This is Dar. Dar likes to work hard, but has had a long day. He had fun at school and at home. Finally, it is time to sleep.

336

Think It Over

 Audio

**Listen to the questions and say the answers.
Use Right Words and Story Words.**

1. What does Mark want to find out?

2. What does blue mean on Mark's globe?

3. What does Star do while Carl eats lunch?

4. Would you like to visit any of the places you read about? Why?

WB
147–148

Reading Strategy

Make Connections

How did making connections help you understand the story?

Grammar and Writing

Adverbs of Time

We use adverbs of time to tell when something happens.

Del has breakfast **before** school.
Del has dinner **after** school.

Use *first*, *then*, *next*, and *finally* to show the order in which things happen.

First, I go to school.
Then I learn about English.
Next, I have lunch.
Finally, I go home.

Use *at*, *on* and *in* with time expressions.

It's **at** 3:00.
It's **on** Monday.
It's **in** October.

338

Practice

Use a word in the box to complete each sentence.

after	before	first	finally	next	then

Example: <u>Then</u> I go to lunch.

1. I eat breakfast ___ school.

2. ___, I walk to my classroom.

3. ___, I listen to the teacher.

4. ___, I go home.

Apply

Tell what you do after school.

Example: A: First, I play with friends. Then I do homework.

   B: After school I visit my dad at work.

Write

Explain what happens on a typical school day.

Before class, the kids talk loudly.
Then the teacher says our names.
We listen to the teacher. Next, we
use the computers.

WB
149–150

THE BIG QUESTION

How are countries alike and different? Talk about it.

Your teacher will help you choose one of these projects.

Written

Write about a favorite country.

Write about a country you would like to visit. Include details that make this country special to you.

Oral

Introduce your favorite country.

Tell the class about your favorite country. Explain what is special about it.

 ## Visual/Active

Draw a favorite country.

Draw a country you have been to or one you would like to visit. Include special sights from that country. Share your drawing with the class.

151–152

Demonstration

Demonstrate how to do a school activity.

❶ Prepare G.O. 112

Think about things you do at school. Choose one.
How would you explain to someone how to do it?
List your ideas in a chart like this:

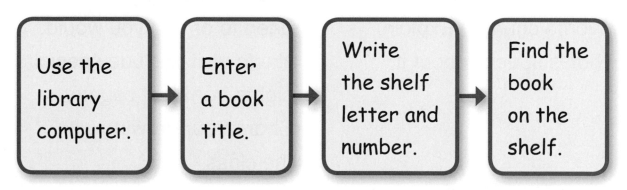

Use the library computer. → Enter a book title. → Write the shelf letter and number. → Find the book on the shelf.

Decide what visuals you can use in your presentation.
Draw a poster or bring props to class.

❷ Practice and Present

Practice with a partner. Use your chart and props.
Then ask your partner if you forgot a step. Next,
when you are ready, act out the steps for the class.
Finally, answer questions from your classmates.

As you speak, do this:

- Speak slowly and use complete sentences.
- Use your props.

As you listen, do this:

- Listen for words you know. This will help you understand.
- Did I understand the speaker's directions?
- Take notes. Write a question if you need information. Later, ask the question.

3 **Evaluate**

Ask yourself these questions:

- Did I tell the steps in order?
- Did I understand my classmates' demonstrations?

> ## Speaking Tip
>
> Use sentences of different lengths and types. Use **and, but,** and **or** correctly.

> ## Listening Tip
>
> The speaker may use the expression "get the hang of." **Getting the hang of** means "becoming good at."

Writing Workshop

Write a How-To Paragraph

Write a paragraph explaining to someone how to make a food from your country.

❶ Prewrite Think about how to make the food. List the steps in order.

José listed the steps of making salsa in this chart.

Step 1: Cut up tomatoes, onion, and garlic.

Step 2: Add lime juice and salt.

Step 3: Add chopped cilantro and peppers.

Step 4: Mix everything in a bowl. Cover and chill.

Step 5: Serve.

❷ Draft Use your graphic organizer to help you write a first draft. Use new words from the unit.

3 **Revise** Read your draft.
Use the Revising Checklist
to correct errors. Then
revise your draft.

Revising Checklist
✓ Are the steps in
  order?

✓ Do I use the
  connecting
  words *and* and
  or correctly?

✓ Do my subjects
  and verbs agree?

Here is José's paragraph.

José Cruz

First, chop five tomatoes one onion,
and a garlic clove. Put the peices into
a bowl. Second, add some lime juice
and salt. Next add chopped cilantro
and jalapeño peppers. Then mix
every thing and chill. Finally, serve
with corn tortilla chips.

4 Edit Trade papers with a partner to get feedback. Use the Editing Checklist.

5 Publish Make a clean copy of your final draft. Share it with the class.

Editing Checklist

✓ The sentences flow smoothly.

✓ The verb tenses are correct.

✓ All words are spelled correctly.

Spelling Tip

The vowel sound in *corn* is also spelled with the pattern *ore*. Examples include *more*, *shore*, *tore*, and *wore*.

For Each Reading...

1. Listen to the sentences.

2. Work in pairs. Take turns reading aloud for one minute. Count the number of words you read.

I will find out about kids from different lands.	9
I will use this globe to see where their homes are.	20
Green means land on this globe and *blue* means	29
water. I will send a note to girls and boys in each	41
country. I will ask them to tell me about their	51
lives. I can ask how boys and girls go to school.	62
Then I can learn what games they play.	70

3. With your partner, find the words that slowed you down. Practice saying each word and then say the sentence each word is in. Then take turns reading the text again. Count the number of words you read.

155–156

A

air

The balloons flew up into the **air**.

animals

Lions are **animals**.

apartment

An **apartment** is a place to live.

are

We **are** on a team.

arms

I have two **arms**.

around

My belt goes **around** my waist.

away

The dog is going **away**.

B

ball

The girl runs with the **ball**.

baseball

I play **baseball**.

348

beach

The **beach** is by the sea.

beautiful

A rainbow is **beautiful**.

beehive

Bees live in a **beehive**.

began

The kids **began** to run when they saw the ice cream truck.

better

Television is **better** today than it was long ago.

big

The box is **big**.

board

The teacher wrote on the **board**.

Gus is in the ____.

born

The baby was **born** this morning.

A
B
C
D
E
F
G
H
I
J
K
L
M
N
O
P
Q
R
S
T
U
V
W
X
Y
Z

A
B
C
D
E
F
G
H
I
J
K
L
M
N
O
P
Q
R
S
T
U
V
W
X
Y
Z

buy

Dan and Gramps **buy** food.

C

cabbage

Cabbage is a green vegetable.

children

The **children** built a sand castle.

chore

I make my bed. I do a **chore**.

clean

I will **clean** the desk.

cold

It is **cold** outside.

continent

A **continent** is a big area of land.

cool

When I am hot, I like to drink **cool** water.

country

Spain is a **country**.

cry

Kids **cry** when they are scared.

D

day

I go out in the **day**.

delicious

Chicken is a **delicious** food.

different

Blue is **different** from red.

does

Does Jed live in an apartment?

done

We rest when we are **done** playing.

down

Dad puts the ball **down**.

A
B
C
D
E
F
G
H
I
J
K
L
M
N
O
P
Q
R
S
T
U
V
W
X
Y
Z

351

E

eat

We **eat** dinner.

ecosystem

A pond is an **ecosystem** where frogs live.

e-mail

I will send you an **e-mail**.

F

family

This is my **family**.

feels

The dog **feels** wet.

five

There are **five** people.

flowers

I like to smell the **flowers**.

found

The squirrel **found** a nut.

friends

Friends play games together.

352

funny

Jen wore a **funny** hat.

give

Give the baby a bottle.

good

Ice cream tastes **good**.

ground

He dug a big hole in the **ground**.

grown-up

My dad is a **grown-up**.

have

I **have** a ball.

heat

I don't like playing outside in this **heat**.

her

Her clothes are clean.

highway

The plane flew over the **highway**.

A
B
C
D
E
F
G
H
I
J
K
L
M
N
O
P
Q
R
S
T
U
V
W
X
Y
Z

him

My dad likes me
to go hiking with **him**.

hold

I **hold** the ball.

horse

Jan rides on a **horse**.

house

I live in a **house**.

hurt

Now Matt will
not get **hurt**.

I

idea

It's a good **idea** to get help from
your parents.

K

keep

My scarf will
keep me warm.

kick

She is going to
kick the ball.

L

lady

My aunt is a
beautiful **lady**.

354

laugh

I **laugh** with my family.

learn

I **learn** at school.

left

There was one piece of cherry pie **left** when I got home.

legacy

Flowers along the roads are the **legacy** that Lady Bird Johnson left us.

letter

The **letter** came in the mail.

light

The baby felt **light**.

M

middle

This man is in the **middle**.

moment

The candles stay lit for a **moment**.

more

The home team has **more** points.

A B C D E F G H I J K L M N O P Q R S T U V W X Y Z

355

A
B
C
D
E
F
G
H
I
J
K
L
M
N
O
P
Q
R
S
T
U
V
W
X
Y
Z

morning

I wake up in
the **morning**.

once

Once I finish
my homework,
I can play!

near

We stand **near** the truck.

only

Only boys go to this school.

nibbles

The mouse **nibbles** on
the cheese.

other

What **other** flavors do you like?

ocelot

An **ocelot** is a beautiful
wild cat.

own

My parents **own**
this house.

356

P

parents

Parents take care of you.

people

Many **people** had fun on the ride.

place

The beach is a great **place** to go with my family.

pool

My neighbors have a **pool** in their backyard.

puppy

A **puppy** is a small dog.

R

river

Trees that need lots of water grow around a **river**.

roads

We cross two **roads** every day.

roost

The hens like to **roost** in nests.

A B C D E F G H I J K L M N O P Q R S T U V W X Y Z

S

said

The girl **said**, "We can make this together."

school

I go to **school** to learn.

shore

It is fun to visit the **shore**.

sign

I can read this **sign**.

simple

Math can be **simple**.

sing

Gramps can **sing**.

small

Berries are **small** fruit.

soccer

He plays **soccer**.

some

Some of the eggs are missing.

soon

I hope the rain stops **soon**.

special

Thanksgiving is a **special** day.

squirrel

The **squirrel** has a big tail.

stay

I will **stay** inside until it stops raining.

students

Students are in a class.

sure

I am **sure** this is a cherry tree.

swans

Many **swans** are white.

T

tasty

Chocolate is a **tasty** treat.

things

We put our **things** on the counter.

A B C D E F G H I J K L M N O P Q R **S T** U V W X Y Z

A B C D E F G H I J K L M N O P Q R S T U V W X Y Z

tofu

Tofu is a healthy snack.

trailer

We live in a **trailer**.

treat

A cookie is a **treat**.

tree

A **tree** can grow tall.

U

under

They sit **under** the umbrella.

V

vegetables

Vegetables are good to eat.

very

I can throw **very** high.

W

waffle

A **waffle** is tasty.

warm

The children are **warm** in their coats and hats.

was

The girl **was** singing.

wash

I **wash** my hands.

water

The boat is on the **water**.

we

We are a family.

who

Who is holding the flowers?

wife

The woman has just become the man's **wife**.

work

We **work** hard in school.

world

Our dream is to travel around the **world**.

would

I **would** like to dance.

Y

year

Twelve months make a **year**.

yellow

His house is **yellow**.

A
B
C
D
E
F
G
H
I
J
K
L
M
N
O
P
Q
R
S
T
U
V
W
X
Y
Z

Index

Credits